I'm getting older, but

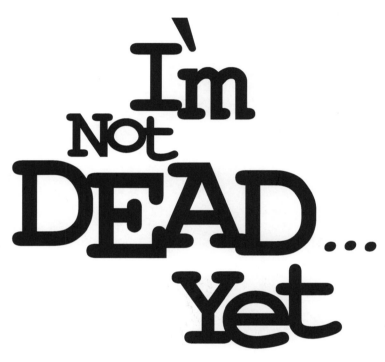

I'm Not DEAD... Yet

and I've got a lot of stuff to do before I die!

A Handbook for Seniors
by John Leslie

D1563861

The little Red Hen
BOOK GROUP

SPRING, TEXAS

Copyright © 2009 by John Leslie

All rights reserved. No part of this book may be reproduced, stored, or transmitted by any means—whether auditory, graphic, mechanical, or electronic—without written permission of both publisher and author, except in the case of brief excerpts used in critical articles and reviews. Unauthorized reproduction of any part of this work is illegal and is punishable by law.

Little Red Hen
Book Group
Spring, Texas

ISBN: 978-0-578-05672-2

Printed in the United States of America
Little Red Hen Book. First printing May, 2010.

ABOUT THE AUTHOR

John Leslie is a retired executive who changed careers after his retirement. He became active in his church, became a lay chaplain, a cancer counselor, an active volunteer helping those who were down on their luck, a "silver-haired" legislator, a charitable institutions board member, and an adult educator developing contemporary issues with morality themes. His goals were to confront and help explain the realities adults were facing in the late 1990's and on.

Along the way he started collecting and writing toasts, attempting to renew in others the joy of celebrating life with friends–aided by modern spirits. His first publishing effort was a compilation of toasts in modern English, **"John Leslie's Little Book of Toasts."**

He has been developing the chapters of this book over the last 10 years. In seminars at the college level to classes for retired seniors, he has guided others in their personal planning for the end of life, polishing and refining topics of interest to those of us over 60. John and his wife, Janice, live in Houston, Texas.

DEDICATION

This book is the result of the efforts of many, many people. . . many whom I've never met. I've researched, studied, attended classes, taught classes, talked, been counseled, had consulting help, and prayed. The result, coupled, luckily, with a few things that I came up with on my own, is this handbook.

The truth is it weren't for the internet and a few dear friends, I'd still be slowly struggling along. My wife, Janice, has encouraged me from the beginning. She watched as others benefited from accepting the challenge of making easier the lives of those who would live on after their death.

In the end, I used everything I could lay my hands on that fit the objectives of this handbook:
- Give seniors an easy-to-follow guide to end-of-life issues
- Reduce some of the natural confusion that occurs as seniors come face to face with the knowledge their death is right around the corner
- Assist in the understanding that death truly is a new beginning, and
- Create loving before-death projects that will make surviving easier for those who are left behind

Writing about dying is a daunting topic. It's scary, too. Preparing for the end of life is not a project many would willingly take on. But there will be an end to life as we know it today. And all of us need help understanding and preparing for it.

I hope you'll find this little handbook helpful. Many seniors who have participated in my seminars did.

Table of Contents

PREFACE

Am I afraid to die?

Yes I am. Of my friends who have died, none have told me what they were doing after they died.

But I know I'm going to die some day. Right now I'm trying to get my life and my stuff in order. While working on this "dying" project, I discovered there were a lot more things to do than I thought. As I talked with others I discovered they, too, recognized the importance of getting their affairs in order but didn't know where to start. From a lot of study and discussions with friends, this handbook evolved.

Dying is like standing in front of a door you've never gone through before, your hand on the door knob, saying to yourself, "I wonder if I'll like what happens to me after I go through?" The problem is, you have to go through the door to find out. And, if you don't like what you find, coming back is probably impossible.

I'm Not Dead Yet is a handbook for seniors who want to get things in shape before they die. It's a practical book, filled with suggestions that have been tried out by lots of people. Some projects are easy, some hard, some may be impossible for you. You'll know yourself better because of these pages, and your survivors will discover you really care for them as they acknowledge all you've done to make their after-your-death lives easier.

You're not dead yet. There are a lot of things for you to do, so let's get started.

It's all about you.
It's about you dying.

Two women met for the first time since graduating from high school.

One asked the other, "You were always so organized in school. How have things gone for you?"

"Well, I've been married four times," was the answer.

"Really?" said her friend.

"My first marriage was to a millionaire; my second marriage was to an actor; my third marriage was to a preacher, and now I'm married to an undertaker."

Curious, her friend asked, "Why did you choose men in those professions?"

"It only makes sense. You know, one for the money, two for the show, three to get ready, and four to go."

It's all about you. It's about you dying. But you're not dead, yet.

Most of us do more for others than we do for ourselves. However in this book everything is about you, a very important person in your universe of loved ones, friends and associates. Although this book concentrates on the practical side of dying, it's not all doom and gloom. Fortunately, many will greatly benefit from what you do as you follow the steps outlined in this handbook.

But make no mistake. This book is for you and about you. You'll be doing things–for yourself–that no one else will do, or, for that matter, could do. And you'll also be doing it all for the people you love.

There are consequences if you don't follow the guidelines of this book. Someone else may attempt to do the very personal things you could have done, but I guarantee that whatever someone else does will not be as good as what you could have done. They will do wonderful things, but the results will not have the stamp of personality that you can give.

Here's an exception: eulogies. You can write your own eulogy and then have someone else read it. You can't capture the thoughts a friend, loved one, or companion would write or speak in a eulogy. You can't know how your life affected another person, try as you may to find out. You're seen in another suit of clothes by others. It may have been an inconsequential act of yours that turned another's life around.

Remember, this is you we're talking about.

GETTING STARTED

Doing all the things this book suggests is hard. You probably won't do them all. In reality, you probably won't do half...right now. You will want to, and some day you'll get around to doing most of them. So, here's the plan.

Put a spiral notebook beside you as you read. On the first page, write, "Going Away." You'll replace that name with one of your choice. (More about that later.) Write the topic title you're currently interested in at the head of another page. Date the page. Follow with any notes you want as you go through the chapters.

On some topics, you'll have many thoughts to jot down. Other topics will require consideration at a later time, or, perhaps, not at all.

Some of the stuff you will want to discuss with a loved one or a friend or a stranger you meet in a coffee shop.

Remember, make a separate page for each topic. And write enough that if you look at the page a month from now, what you've written will bring back a thought or two. The importance of doing this will become increasingly apparent as you go through the book.

I believe that developing answers to the items listed in the forms in the "Instant Action" chapter of this book will change your life. If you respond to every one of the topics in that chapter you will become a legend within your family. Your heirs will tell stories about you for generations.

Following are examples from the "Instant Action" chapter. Take a look at them. You'll be reading a lot more about them later on, but for now, "Instant Action" means this is the piece of paper people will turn to right after you die. It's obvious information is quickly needed at the time of your death. It has to be developed by someone...better by you than anyone else. It starts with developing answers to questions like these:

- ☐ Family members to notify *(other persons to be notified are listed on my "People I Want to be Notified of my Death" form; some can be emailed, others called or written to)*

- ☐ Minister to call

- ☐ Two close friends to call for support to my survivors

- ☐ Call Hospice *(if they have been involved)*

- ☐ This person knows what I want done with my body

- ☐ Funeral home or crematory and phone number to call to remove my body *(in case of an unusual circumstance like an accident, crime or suicide, the coroner's or sheriff's office should first be called)*

- ☐ Where my burial instructions can be found

- ☐ Doctor to certify death

- ☐ Personal attorney

- ☐ CPA/Financial advisor

- ☐ Life insurance agent

- ☐ Where more "needed information" can be found

OK. We're about ready to start.

One last word. There may be some topics in this book that bore you to tears. But stick with me. There's no other book I know of that is as straight talking and inclusive as this. You may not like one subject, but the next chapter may be about something that has concerned you all your life.

Take the quiz that follows: "Checking your attitude about end-of-life issues." It will help you understand how important a task you're taking on and you'll begin to see how your life is about to be changed.

As I've said before, it's a little scary, too.

CHECKING YOUR ATTITUDE ABOUT END-OF-LIFE ISSUES

- ☐ How many more years do you think you will live?
- ☐ Do you think having a plan for the end of your life will be helpful to your loved ones? Why?
- ☐ Name one end-of-life decision you could make now.
- ☐ As you think about dying, what bothers you the most?
- ☐ Name at least 3 persons you will want to inform of your end-of-life plans.
- ☐ Does your family know your preferences for burial or cremation?
- ☐ Do you fear dying? Or the pain that precedes death?
- ☐ What is the most important memory of yourself you will leave behind?
- ☐ How are you going to pass on such gifts as your wisdom, faith, and understanding of life?
- ☐ If you were responsible for planning the closure of the life of another, what information do you think would be most helpful?

THE REALITIES OF AGING

As you age, there are events that everyone older can relate to and about which you can talk with almost anyone:

- ☐ I have aches and pains I didn't have 10 years ago
- ☐ My medicine is so expensive
- ☐ I don't sleep well any more
- ☐ My sex life isn't what it used to be

And on and on....And, as you begin to accept that you are declining a little, you ask:

☐ Should we sell our house?

☐ Should we move into a retirement village or an apartment?

If your health is failing, the question becomes:

☐ Should I have Home Health Care or move into an Assisted Living Facility?

If your health is really going down hill:

☐ Should I move to an Extended Care Facility?

It's pretty normal to have an "attitude" about getting older. If it weren't so troublesome, it'd almost be funny.

It was fun being a baby boomer. . . until now. Some of the artists of the 60's are revising their hits with new titles and lyrics to accommodate us aging baby boomers:

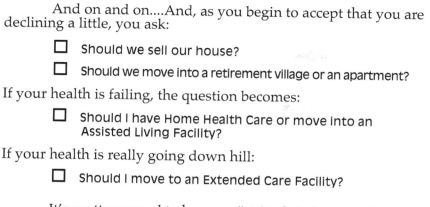

Herman's Hermits – Mrs. Brown, You've Got a Lovely Walker
Ringo Starr – I Get By With a Little Help From Depends
The Bee Gees – How Can You Mend a Broken Hip?
Bobby Darin – Splish, Splash, I Was Havin' a Flash
Roberta Flack – The First Time Ever I Forgot Your Face
Johnny Nash – I Can't See Clearly Now
Paul Simon – Fifty Ways to Lose Your Liver
The Commodores – Once, Twice, Three Times to the Bathroom
Leo Sayer – You Make Me Feel Like Napping
The Temptations – Papa's Got a Kidney Stone
Tony Orlando – Knock 3 Times On Your Ceiling If You Hear Me Fall
Helen Reddy – I Am Woman, Hear Me Snore

We'll be discussing an even-more frightening subject than aging–dying–a little further on. Far too few people appreciate what a wonderful gift thoughtful end-of-life planning is. Lack of planning will leave your loved ones feeling emotionally and financially hijacked.

Luckily, as we age, there's always something to laugh about. George Carlin, the famous comedian, shared his views on aging:

Do you realize that the only time in our lives when we like to get old is when we're kids? If you're less than 10 years old, you're so excited about aging that you think in fractions.

How old are you?
"I'm four and a half!" You're never thirty-six and a half. You're four and a half, going on five! That's the key.

You get into your teens, now they can't hold you back. You jump to the next number, or even a few ahead.

How old are you? "I'm gonna be 16!" You could be 13, but hey, you're gonna be 16!

And then the greatest day of your life . . you become 21 . . . Even the words sound like a ceremony . . .YOU BECOME 21. YESSSS!!!

But then you turn 30. Oooohh, what happened there? Makes you sound like bad milk! He TURNED; we had to throw him out. There's no fun now, you're just a sour dumping. What's wrong? What's changed?

You BECOME 21, you TURN 30, then you're PUSHING 40. Whoa! Put on the brakes. It's all slipping away. Before you know it, you REACH 50 and your dreams are gone.

But wait!!! You MAKE it to 60. You didn't think you would!

So you BECOME 21, TURN 30, PUSH 40, REACH 50 and MAKE it to 60.

You've built up so much speed that you HIT 70! After that it's a day-by-day thing. You HIT Wednesday!

You get into your 80s and every day is a complete cycle; you HIT lunch; you TURN 4:30; you REACH bedtime. And it doesn't end there. Into the 90s, you start going backwards. 'I Was JUST 92.'

Then a strange thing happens. If you make it over 100, you become a little kid again. I'm 100 and a half!

May you all make it to a healthy 100 and a half!

There are many things we have an interest in as we age that we never gave a minute's thought to when we were in our 40's. Our age is one of them. As young adults, we thought we were bullet proof and would live forever. Not so any more. Any topic that indicates it will help us get a few more good years is worth a second look.

SOME INTERESTING FACTS FOR OLDER PERSONS:

- Excessive coffee can both indicate and exacerbate stress.
- Research shows that chronic gum disease leads to the release of inflammatory substances and bacteria into the blood stream and can lead to heart disease.
- Radon is a gas emitted from various types of rock, especially granite, and can accumulate to dangerous levels in people's homes.
- Exercise leads to more efficient energy production and lowers the production of age accelerating free radicals in our cells.
- Diabetes causes excessive exposure to glucose and, when uncontrolled, results in the earlier onset of age-related problems.
- Charring food can change proteins and amino acids into carcinogens.
- Cigarette smoke contains toxins that directly damage DNA and subsequently cause cancer.
- Some studies suggest that 90 percent of all human cancers are environmentally produced, 30 to 40 percent of these by diet.
- High protein diets, and the combination of a high fat and protein diet, have been associated with increased risk of many types of cancer.
- A number of air pollutants are potent causes of cancer and contain oxidants that accelerate aging.
- Excessive alcohol is toxic.
- Viruses such as HIV and others that are transmitted by risky behavior, not only cause AIDS but also various cancers, including lymphoma.
- The association between sun exposure and accelerated skin aging is clear.
- Extended family cohesiveness and frequent contact is a notable feature of centenarian families.

- Centenarians shed emotional stress exceptionally well.
- Obesity is associated with inefficient energy production.
- Genetics play a significant role in the ability to achieve extreme old age.
- Vitamin E is thus far the best scientifically proven antioxidant available either in the diet or as a dietary supplement.
- The ultraviolet rays in sunlight directly damage DNA.
- Toxic levels of radon in the home are equivalent to smoking two packs of cigarettes a day.
- Exercise has been linked to lower rates of breast and prostate cancer.
- Keeping gut transit time under 20 hours seems to decrease the incidence of colon cancer.
- If you have significant extreme longevity in your family, it will help significantly in your own ability to achieve old age in good health.
- Selenium appears to have dramatic effects in preventing cancer.
- Only 36% of male baby boomers exercise regularly.
- Only 35% of female baby boomers exercise regularly.
- Centenarians preserve their cognitive function by engaging in mental activities that are interesting to them.

Good health is an essential part of good living and is really important in determining how long you will live. An important step in keeping your body healthy and functional is to regularly evaluate how you are doing and then adjust appropriately.

HOW'RE YOU DOING PERSONALLY?

The "Healthspan Calculator," developed by longevity researchers at Harvard Medical School and Boston Medical Center, is a great tool to quickly assess what you are doing right and wrong, and to identify your biggest health risks.

A questionnaire based on the Healthspan Calculator test questions follows. Answering the questions and then analyzing your answers will give you a petty good indication of what's happening to you now and where you're headed. If you're interested, additional good information can be found at the Alliance for Aging Research web page, *www.agingresearch.org*.

In terms of living to older age in good health, there are actually a great many things you can do to improve your life expectancy. The quiz will highlight some of those things and also help you determine your approximate life expectancy.

A. Personal Information

1. What is your gender? ☐ Male ☐ Female
2. Your age:
3. What is your marital status?
   ☐ Single, ☐ Married, ☐ Divorced, ☐ Widowed
4. Do your family members–other then your spouse and children–live near enough to spontaneously drop by?
   ☐ Yes
   ☐ No
   ☐ Don't have any family
5. How do you evaluate your current stress level (*within the last 12 months*)?
   ☐ Low
   ☐ Medium
   ☐ High
6. How do you usually cope with your stress?
   ☐ Very well! It helps me to get motivated.
   ☐ Good! I can shed stress by using techniques that reduce stress (*meditation, exercise, etc.*).
   ☐ I am doing all right! I am trying to find ways to protect myself from it.
   ☐ Not very good! Stress eats away at me and I can't seem to shake it off.
7. How many hours of sleep do you usually get per night?
   ☐ 3 to 5 hours
   ☐ 5 to 8 hours
   ☐ Over 8 hours

8. How would you characterize your sleep habits?

☐ Very good! I sleep enough and through the night.
☐ It varies. I have sleepless nights once in while.
☐ It's OK. My sleep could certainly be better.
☐ Very bad. Every night I have problems falling or staying asleep.

9. What's your physical constitution?

10. How much do you weigh?

11. How tall are you?

B. Lifestyle Habits/Environmental Circumstances

1. How is the air quality (air pollution) where you live?

☐ Very bad. *(Industrial area/ lots of smog)*
☐ Average. *(Urban area/ medium smog)*
☐ Okay. *(Suburbs/ low smog)*
☐ Very good. *(Countryside/ no smog)*

2. How often do you put your seat belt on when you are in a car (either as driver or passenger)?

☐ Always
☐ About 80% of the time
☐ Half of the time
☐ Less than half of the time

3. How many cups of coffee do you drink per day?

☐ None
☐ 1 to 2 cups
☐ Over 3 cups

4. How often do you drink tea?

☐ Never
☐ Rarely
☐ Sometimes
☐ Daily

5. Do you smoke or are you exposed to second-hand smoke?

☐ Yes   ☐ No

6. If your answer was "Yes," what is your daily tobacco exposure? *(cigarettes, cigars, pipe, chewing tobacco)*?

☐ Daily
☐ Not daily, but often
☐ Sometimes
☐ Rarely or never

7. If you don't smoke, what is your exposure to close-proximity second-hand smoke?

☐ Daily
☐ Not daily, but often
☐ Sometimes
☐ Rarely or never

8. How many days per week do you usually consume alcohol?

☐ I don't drink alcohol
☐ 1 or 2 days per week
☐ 3 to 5 days per week
☐ Every day of the week

9. On the days you drink alcoholic beverages *(beer, wine or mixed drinks)*, how many glasses do you usually drink?

☐ I don't drink
☐ 1 - 2
☐ 2 - 3
☐ Over 3

10. How often do you take an aspirin or an over-the-counter anti-inflammatory medication *(Motrin/Advil)?*

☐ Never
☐ Occasionally
☐ Frequently
☐ Every day

11. Do you wear sun screen (at least SPF 30) or protective clothing when you spend time in the sun?

☐ Rarely or never
☐ Sometimes
☐ Most of the time
☐ Always

12. Do you engage in risky sexual (unprotected) or drug-related behavior?

☐ Never
☐ Sometimes
☐ Often
☐ Very often

13. Besides brushing your teeth, do you also floss your teeth every day?

☐ Yes ☐ No

C. Nutrition & Exercise

1. How many servings of processed meats or fast foods *(like hot dogs, bologna, etc.)* do you eat a week?

☐ None
☐ 1 - 2 servings
☐ 3 - 4 servings
☐ Over 5 servings

2. How do you barbecue fish, poultry, or meat?

☐ I am a vegetarian
☐ I never barbecue
☐ I put aluminum foil on the grill
☐ Lightly grilled and still juicy
☐ Well done, almost charred

3. How many servings of dairy products (milk, cheese, yogurt, etc.) do you eat per day? *(Example for 1 serving: 1 cup of milk, 1 cup of yogurt, or 1/2 oz. cheese).*

☐ 0 - 1 servings
☐ 2 - 3 servings
☐ More than 3 servings

4. I also take supplemental calcium.

☐ Yes ☐ No

5. Do you snack between meals?

☐ Yes ☐ No

6. If you do snack between meals, generally which of the following are your snacks? Choose all that apply.

☐ Fruit   ☐ Yogurt   ☐ Veggies
☐ Candies ☐ Chocolate ☐ Cookies
☐ Bagel   ☐ Chips   ☐ Crackers
☐ Popcorn
☐ "Healthy" drink *(e.g., fruit based, teas, etc.)*
☐ "Unhealthy" drinks *(e.g., popular sodas)*

7. How often per week do you have meat as your main course?
   - ☐ I don't eat meat
   - ☐ I eat meat 1-2 days per week
   - ☐ I eat meat 3-5 days per week
   - ☐ I eat meat 6-7 days per week

8. How often to you eat sweets such as ice cream, cake/pie/ pastry, or candy bars?
   - ☐ I avoid sweets
   - ☐ 1-2 days per week
   - ☐ 3-5 days per week
   - ☐ Once a day
   - ☐ More than once per day

9. What about carbohydrates like white bread or rolls, potatoes, French fries, pasta, white rice? How often do you have at least one serving of one of these?
   - ☐ 1 or fewer servings a week
   - ☐ 1 serving twice a week
   - ☐ 1 serving every other day
   - ☐ 1-2 servings a day
   - ☐ 3 or more servings a day

10. Do you believe you have a diet that leads to weight gain or do you eat an amount of calories that either maintains weight or is actually conducive to healthy weight loss?
    - ☐ I eat too much everyday, making it easy for me to stay overweight or to gain even more weight
    - ☐ I have a diet in which I am losing weight with a target of a healthy weight
    - ☐ I am maintaining a healthy weight with the diet I currently have

11. Do you take vitamin E every day *(200-1000 IU per day)*?
    - ☐ Yes ☐ No

12. Do you take Iron either as a supplement or part of a multivitamin?
    - ☐ Yes ☐ No

13. How many days a week do you exercise *(strength training, aerobic exercises or activities such as swimming, running, and biking)* for at least 30 minutes a day?

☐ 7 days per week   ☐ 6 days per week
☐ 5 days per week   ☐ 3 days per week
☐ 2 days per week   ☐ 1 day per week
☐ I don't exercise

D. Medical Check-up

1. Do you have a bowel movement at least once every two days?

☐ Yes   ☐ No

I have a bowel movement less frequently than every two days

☐ Yes   ☐ No

2. Female: Do you regularly screen for cancer *(skin and breasts)* by doing self-examinations?

☐ Yes   ☐ No

Male: Do you regularly screen for cancer *(skin and testicles)* by doing self-examinations?

☐ Yes   ☐ No

3. What is your cholesterol level and your triglyceride level?

HDL cholesterol *(good cholesterol)*:

☐ Lower than 35 mg/dl
☐ Higher than 35 mg/dl
☐ I haven't checked it in the last 3 years
☐ I have had the test done within the past 3 years but don't remember the results

LDL cholesterol (bad cholesterol):

☐ Lower than 130 mg/dl
☐ Higher than 130 mg/dl
☐ I haven't checked it in the last 3 years
☐ I have had the test done within the past 3 years but don't remember the results

Triglyceride level:

☐ Lower than 145 mg/dl
☐ Higher than 145 mg/dl
☐ I haven't checked it in the last 3 years
☐ I have had the test done within the past 3 years but don't remember the results

4. What is your systolic and diastolic blood pressure? (*The systolic pressure is always stated first and diastolic pressure second. For example: 122/76 (122 over 76); systolic = 122, diastolic = 76).* If you don't know your blood pressure, go to the "I haven't checked" option

Systolic blood pressure *(higher value):*

☐ Lower than 85   ☐ 86-100

☐ 101-129   ☐ 130-139

☐ 140-189   ☐ 190-210

☐ 211-230   ☐ Higher than 230

Diastolic blood pressure (*lower value*):

☐ Lower than 80   ☐ 80-89

☐ 90-105 ☐ 106-115

☐ Higher than 116

☐ I have not had my blood pressure checked in the past 3 years

5. Do you have diabetes?

☐ Yes ☐ No

6. What is your fasting blood sugar level?

☐ I have not had it checked in the past 3 years

☐ No diabetes

☐ 120-200

☐ >200

7. When did you have your last doctor's appointment for your regular medical check-up (which includes blood pressure check, age-and gender-appropriate screening, immunizations, review of medical history, and analysis about your risk factors)?

☐ My last preventive care visit was over 3 years ago.

☐ My last preventive care visit was between 1- 3 years ago.

☐ My last preventive care visit was within the past year.

E. Family History

1. Do you know the health history of your immediate family members?

2. How many members of your immediate family (parents and siblings) have diabetes?

   ☐ None ☐ One ☐ Two
   ☐ Three and more: ☐ Don't know

3. Does cancer run in your family?

   ☐ Yes ☐ No

4. How many non-smoking members of your immediate family (grandparents, parents, siblings) were diagnosed with cancer (other than benign skin cancers)?

   ☐ None ☐ One ☐ Two
   ☐ Three and more: ☐ Don't know

5. How old and how healthy are/were your parents? (For your mother and father give one answer each.)

   Mother:

   ☐ Under the age of 80/ healthy
   ☐ Prior to age 80/ mother has or died of a smoking related illness (cancer, heart attack, stroke, emphysema)
   ☐ Under the age of 80/ dependent on others
   ☐ Over the age of 80/ healthy
   ☐ Over the age of 80/ dependent on others
   ☐ Died before age 80
   ☐ Died age 80-89
   ☐ Died age 90-99
   ☐ Died age 100 or older
   ☐ Adopted, don't know

   Father:

   ☐ Under the age of 80/ healthy
   ☐ Prior to age 80/ father has or died of a smoking related illness (cancer, heart attack, stroke, emphysema)
   ☐ Under the age of 80/ dependent on others
   ☐ Over the age of 80/ healthy
   ☐ Over the age of 80/ dependent on others
   ☐ Died before age 80
   ☐ Died age 80-89
   ☐ Died age 90-99

☐   Died age 100 or older

☐   Adopted, don't know

6. In terms of longevity in your family, did any of your grandparents or siblings of your parents live beyond the age of 94 years?

☐   Yes   ☐   No

Women only: How old were you when you last had a child without fertility/technology assistance?

☐   I have not had any children

☐   Younger than 35

☐   35-39

☐   40-45

☐   >45

Based on your answers to these questions, summarize below your life span probabilities. Write your conclusions for each section in your notebook.

> **Personal Information:** *(Did the Personal Information indicate any potential problems?)*
>
> **Lifestyle:** *(Is your lifestyle dangerous?)*
>
> **Nutrition and Exercise:** *(Are you in shape for your age?)*
>
> **Medical History:** *(Have you healthily adjusted to your age?)*
>
> **Family History:** *(Based on how long your family members lived, how many more years do you think you will live?)*

All the tests, comments, and bad jokes are intended to emphasize the reality that life is sometimes ordinary, sometimes funny, sometimes stressed, and sometimes serious. Hopefully, recognizing that change is normal, it then is easier to address the questions: "How much longer do I have to live? What is the quality of my life?" A grin or a laugh may make the answer a little easier to take. Finally, you'll be better able to prepare for your death if you can find a way to laugh at reality.

LIFE EXPECTANCY

Life expectancy is the average life span for an individual. Life expectancy figures are collected by national health systems that then project current mortality statistics. Life expectancy is generally given for a person based on the year they were born. But this estimate is tricky, because life expectancy changes based on age and gender.

LIFE EXPECTANCY AT BIRTH

For persons born in 2009, the U.S. life expectancy is 77.5 years. This number takes the current rates of mortality at each age and figures out the average. Deaths at young ages impact life expectancy averages much more than older deaths. If a person dies at 18, 59.5 years of life expectancy are lost. A person dying at age 70 only loses 7.5 years. Young deaths impact life expectancy "at birth" statistics. Reducing your risk to the most common causes of death of young people, such as car accidents, will significantly increase your "at birth" life expectancy.

LIFE EXPECTANCY AT 65

As people age, their life expectancy actually increases. Each year you live means that you have survived all sorts of potential causes of death. A person born in 1942 and alive in 2006 had a life expectancy at birth of about 68 years. But the good news is that since you didn't die of infectious diseases when young, car accidents, or anything else, you can expect to live another 18.4 years. So your life expectancy now is not the same as it was at your birth. It is 5.9 years longer than the current life expectancy figure for people born in 2006, or 83 .4 years.

LIFE EXPECTANCY AT 75

The news just keeps getting better. If you make it to 75, your life expectancy increases to 86.8 years. You gain another 3.4 years. That means the average 75-year old will live 9.3 years longer than the average child born in 2006.

Sound like funny math? It's not; it is one of those weird things that statistics does. So don't be disappointed when you outlive the current average life expectancy at birth. Only the oldest person in the world can outlive his or her own life expectancy. For the rest of us, there is always someone older.

GENDER DIFFERENCES

Men tend to die younger, bringing down the averages. The average 65 year old woman today can expect to live another 19.8 years or a total of 84.8 years. If she makes it to 75, she can expect an additional 12.6 years or a total of 87.6 years. Men don't do quite as well, but the difference shrinks as they age. A 75 year old man can expect, on average, another 10.5 years or 85.5 years total. Remember, these are averages –you can beat them by eating right, staying active, staying involved and exercising your brain.

So, what do you think now? What's your educated best guess as to how long you'll live? Additional good information can be found at *www.agingresearch.org.*

Before ending this chapter, here are a few more statistics that show the improvements medical science and nutrition have made that are increasing our life expectancy:

In 1950 the life expectancy:

- at birth was: 68.2
- for 65 year olds: 78.9
- for 75 year olds: no data available

In 1980 the life expectancy:

- at birth was: 73.7
- for 65 year olds: 81.4
- for 75 year olds: 85.4

In 2003 the life expectancy:

- at birth was: 77.5
- for 65 year olds: 83.4
- for 75 year olds: 86.8

In 2005 the leading causes of death were:

- Diseases of heart *(heart disease)*
- Malignant neoplasms *(cancer)*
- Cerebrovascular diseases *(stroke)*
- Chronic lower respiratory diseases
- Accidents *(unintentional injuries)*
- Diabetes mellitus (diabetes)
- Alzheimer

Source: CDC -- Health, United States, 2006

Make no mistake. Regardless of what they do to enable us to live longer, eventually, we will die.

Are you ready?

It's time to make the numbers work for you. Hopefully, you can say, "I believe that after my death wonderful things will happen to me in another place. I also understand the friends and loved ones I've left behind will experience loss–emotional and physical loss–at my death."

This book is for those of us who want to lessen the trauma that will occur with our death. It's practical for both companions to prepare their "Going Away" book together, for much of the information applies to each.

This book is a compilation of what has been learned from working with lots of people and the "best practices" we've jointly developed. *I believe, as do the persons who have made this journey with me, that the methodology we have developed will make "survivorship" less painful.*

Of course, nothing we can do will replace the void caused by death.

When a person dies, there are thousands of details that must be attended to by somebody. Coupled with the pain of loss, there is the stress created by having to perform unfamiliar tasks. Anything that can be done to help is a plus. Following the blueprint of this book, dying becomes a part of life that can be handled.

The process starts with things you can do while you're still alive and kicking–things that if you didn't do, someone else would have to do after your death. All you have to do is recognize the importance of advance preparation and accept the fact that death is a normal part of life.

As we've seen, you and I are living longer. The accepted future norm is that, by 2030, 1 of 5 Americans will be 65 or older. My wife and I see this happening where we live in Harris County, Texas. It's estimated that by 2020 there will be about 670,000 persons 60 years old or older living in Harris county. Ten years ago there were about 475,000 persons 60 years old or older in the county. An increase of almost 200,000 in 10 years indicates good medical care, good living standards, good retirement, a worry-free life style, and luck.

Living longer gives us opportunity to do things. When retired and assured of an income, we have a tendency to spread out *(I don't mean "gaining weight" spread out, but, unfortunately, that happens too!)* and do the things we have wanted to do all our lives but couldn't because we had to work. Later on you'll write the things you want to do before you die. There are lots of great examples of the accomplishments of older citizens.

Even though we live longer, there is a day when we will die. Every one of us is moving towards the time our death will occur. It's not something to complain about. I hope you understand that death is a normal part of the life cycle. We just don't want to die a slow, painful death, do we?

Dying is not a subject we like to talk about. And, if you talk about it a lot, people will think you've "got a problem." So, out of consideration for our friends and family, many of us put off the important decisions and depend on others to make them after we're gone. That's not fair.

Today, life can be roughly divided into thirds, the first third occurring from age 1 to 30. The second part is from 31 to 60, and the third from 61 to 90. There's no doubt we are living longer and accomplishing more.

That's good.

Your Going AWAY Book

We all react differently to change

A mother, father, and their son were visiting the Mall of America for the first time. In fact, it was the first time they had ever been outside their small rural community.

The father saw an elevator door open (he really didn't know what an elevator did). A large woman got on, the doors closed, and he watched the elevator rise to the fourth floor.

After a minute, the elevator came back down to the first floor, the doors opened and a slim, attractive young woman came out.

The father nudged his son and said, "Quick, son, go get your mother!"

Too few people appreciate what a wonderful gift thoughtful end-of–life planning can be. Your death represents change that cannot be imagined. Lack of preparation will leave your loved ones feeling emotionally and financially hijacked. Don't leave them that way.

IT'S HARD TO TALK ABOUT DEATH AND DYING

When you've gone through all the chapters in this book you'll have a sensible and practical approach to the events associated with your death. The result of reading and doing the things these chapters discuss ends up in a book of your own that is described in this chapter.

Getting a companion or one of your children to willingly talk about "death" is quite an accomplishment. The topic isn't easily brought into any conversation. The first time you do it look out for squirming, glazed eyes, hands that can't stay still, hopeful looks that a cell phone will ring, etc. The second time may result in mayhem!

Do you find it hard to talk about your death? What are your expectations about the process that leads to your dying? If you were suffering a lot, what would you want the doctors to do?

Early on, try to be open about the subject of dying. Being comfortable talking about it is more difficult. Achieving both those objectives is not easy. Telling a joke or a humorous story takes the edge off, so there are times when a chuckle seems indicated. Humor will enable you to leap over any hurdles that might keep you from a reasonable and sensible evaluation of the needs of those who will live on after your death. Hopefully, you will soon be filled with a spirit of freedom and be able to accept and talk about death as a natural ending to life, one that will happen to all of us.

When a person becomes aware that the end is approaching, a statement, "I want to talk about dying because that's what I'm doing right now," makes sense. Hearing it said may create a feeling of inadequacy. Whether you are the one dying or the one listening to the person who is dying, don't enter the process by manufacturing a phony, upbeat attitude. But don't be doom and gloom either!

Neglecting to face life's end's realities can have disastrous consequences. Neglect could easily create serious financial problems and other emotional and relationship issues. Get over the thought that talking about and making decisions about death while you're still alive is disrespectful. Wisdom is needed and is often in short supply when death occurs in your own family. Absence of a pre-planned, thoughtful closure to the dying process involves enormous repercussions for the survivors. Being informed about the complexities of decisions and the available possibilities enable you to make better choices. Believe me; you'll be glad you know about these things.

Your death is a once-in-a lifetime occurrence! The memories surrounding your end-of-life adventure will be discussed for years after you are gone.

DO YOU KNOW THE ANSWERS?

- Have you ever brought up the subject of your dying with your family?
- What did they say?
- If asked, what would they say they'd do on your death? Is it a subject that is taboo in your home?
- Are there parts of your life *(or others in your family)* that you want to be sure someone knows about?
- Do you have stories you want to share?
- Do your survivors know the minister to notify of your death?
- Do they know whether you want to be cremated or buried?
- Do they know where you want your body or ashes to be buried or your ashes to be scattered?
- What kind of a funeral or memorial service do you want?
- Is there a specific doctor to call to verify your death?
- Who are the first persons to be notified of your death?
- What do you want your obituary to say?
- Where is your will?
- What do you want done with your household goods?
- How are your personal possessions to be divided?
- Have you identified and marked your possessions you will give away?
- Does anyone else have authorization to your strong box?
- Does your family know about emergency funds that will keep bills paid until your estate is settled?
- Are there other persons who can sign on your checking accounts?
- Have you given anyone authority to dispose of your assets?

Can you see the advantage of deciding some of this stuff in advance? The more you think and talk about death, the easier it gets. However, don't talk about it so much that you become a bore!

The questions that can be asked never end. Here are some more:

- Have you identified the goals you have for the rest of your life?
- Are there things you have to accomplish before you die?
- Are there places you want to go?
- Have you thought about whose feelings might be hurt if they don't get that something "special" after your death?
- What do you want done if you cannot make medical or personal decisions for yourself?
- Have you prepared a list of people *(and their addresses)* you want notified of your death?

CHECKING YOUR ATTITUDE ABOUT END-OF-LIFE ISSUES

Following is the little questionnaire you took in Chapter 1. It was intended to put a perspective on your eventual death. Without looking back, answer the questions again and then compare your answers.

- How many more years do you think you will live?
- How will planning for the end of your life be helpful to you and your loved ones?
- Name one end-of-life decision you could make now?
- As you think about dying, what bothers you the most?
- Name three persons you will want to inform about your end-of-life plans?
- Does your family know your preferences about burial or cremation?
- If you were in great pain, what would you want the doctors to do?
- What memory of yourself would you like to leave behind?
- How can you best pass on such gifts as your wisdom, faith, and understanding of life?
- If you were responsible for planning the closure of the life of another, what information do you think would be most helpful?

It makes sense to bring order to what now probably appears to be a confused mess.

To start, you need a place to file your decisions, financial information, personal, legal, and historical data. There are hundreds of topics of importance you need to put somewhere so that, after you die, others will be able to find them. You need a "Going Away" book to put all that stuff in.

WHAT'S A "GOING AWAY" BOOK?

Think of it like this: when you die, someone *(one of the three or more persons you have informed about your end-of-life plans and who know the location of your book)* will pull the book off the shelf, open the first section, "Instant Action," and know what to do because you've spelled it all out.

TOPICS YOU MAY WANT TO INCLUDE IN YOUR "GOING AWAY" BOOK

What will you put in your Going Away book? Your book is your personal document and you will want in it the material that will be most helpful to your survivors. There are, however, some universal subjects that everyone would want to have in their Going Away book. Things like:

- ☐ Advance Directives
- ☐ Attorney
- ☐ Bank Accounts
- ☐ Birth Certificates
- ☐ Brokerage Accounts
- ☐ Burial or Cremation Information
- ☐ Car Titles
- ☐ Caregivers
- ☐ Cemetery/Columbarium Information
- ☐ Cherished Possessions *(to be given away)* and their Stories
- ☐ Church Contacts
- ☐ Debts that are recorded and debts that are not recorded
- ☐ Family History
- ☐ Financial Advisors/Information
- ☐ Funeral Home to use

- ☐ Hospice if you need it
- ☐ Insurance Policies
- ☐ Inventory of Items to be given away that are not listed in your will, are not cherished possessions, and how they will be disposed of
- ☐ Inventory of Items to bequeathed that are listed in your will
- ☐ Loans
- ☐ Long-Term Care Instructions
- ☐ Marriage License
- ☐ Military Papers
- ☐ Funeral/Memorial Service Notes
- ☐ People to Notify of Serious Illness or Death
- ☐ Physicians
- ☐ Prescriptions/Vitamins, etc.
- ☐ Real Estate Titles/Mortgages
- ☐ Social Security/ Medicare
- ☐ Things I Want to Do before I Die
- ☐ What to Do When My Death Occurs notes
- ☐ Will

When you begin thinking about it, there are many, many topics that become important to others when you're no longer around. This is your list; add or delete entries and write your choices in your notebook. And the list is never final; any time you think of something you believe others should know about, stick it in your book.

INSTANT ACTION

Not listed in the above list is one topic of critical importance: "Instant Action." The documents you put in this section will contain the answers to the immediate decision requirements death creates– decisions that have to be made quickly. If many of those decisions were anticipated and made in advance, the pain and confusion your survivors will experience at your death will be substantially reduced.

So, does the logic of getting everything in order and in one place make sense? Of course it does. So begin the process right now that will enable your survivors to follow your instructions rather than having to make decision they're unprepared to make. Start preparing your book. Give it a name. Start putting things in your book knowing the information will eliminate some of the emotional stress your death creates along with the pressures to make "right" decisions.

NAMING YOUR BOOK AND PUTTING IT TOGETHER

I humorously named my Going Away book, "One for the Money, Two for the Show, Three to Get Ready, and Four to Go." You can name your book anything.

I put divider tabs in a big three-ring notebook and wrote my choices of book section titles on five of the tabs:

- Instant Action (*instructions regarding what to do right after I've died*)
- One for the Money (*financial and legal information*)
- Two for the Show (*information that should be shown and discussed with others*)
- Three to Get Ready (*end of life decisions*)
- Four to Go (*funeral/memorial plans*)

Then I took the list of topics from my spiral notebook and put them into groups that fit the sectional headings above. You'll see below how I put the details together. There's no "right" way. Use some creativity. . . and humor.

CONTENTS OF A TYPICAL GOING AWAY BOOK

Here's the listing of the contents of my personal book. My outline shows the way I chose to put information and forms behind each tab. Remember, it's your book, so if you don't like where I've put a topic, put it where you want it.

INSTANT ACTION (*More on this later*)

ONE FOR THE MONEY
- ☐ Brokerage Accounts
- ☐ Loans
- ☐ Bank Accounts
- ☐ Financial Information
- ☐ Real Estate Titles/Mortgages
- ☐ Attorney
- ☐ Birth Certificates
- ☐ Car Titles
- ☐ Insurance Policies

TWO FOR THE SHOW

- ☐ Prescriptions/Vitamins, etc.
- ☐ Social Security/ Medicare
- ☐ Physicians and Caregivers
- ☐ Marriage License

THREE TO GET READY

- ☐ Advance Directives
- ☐ Letters of Permission
- ☐ Inventory of Items to Be Given Away
- ☐ Cherished Possessions and Their Stories
- ☐ Military Papers
- ☐ Things I Want to Do before I Die
- ☐ Family History
- ☐ Hospice
- ☐ Long-Term Care Instructions

FOUR TO GO

- ☐ Cemetery/Columbarian Information
- ☐ Funeral/Memorial Service
- ☐ Will and Loving Letters
- ☐ Advance Directives
- ☐ Burial/Cremation Information
- ☐ Going-Away Party
- ☐ Church Contacts
- ☐ People to Notify of Serious Illness or Death

The chapters in this book describe the process of creating your very own Going Away book, the contents of which can be similar to those described above.

Have you chosen a name for your book yet? (*A little later on I'll show you the names others have chosen for their book. You'll agree, I think, that the titles reflect some very creative minds!*)

A CHECKLIST FOR YOUR GOING AWAY BOOK

As you start gathering the information you will need for your book, it will help to have a checklist of the documents you will collect. This is different list from the sections in the various chapters in your book *(like "Instant Action")*. It's a topical list. Topical Lists show specific data, forms, or documents. Like all the other parts of the book, personalize it to your satisfaction. Add to or change a topical list as you think of things–you can rearrange them anyway you want to. Here's an example:

- ☐ Birth certificate
- ☐ Auto registration
- ☐ Baptismal certificate
- ☐ Homeowners insurance policy
- ☐ Marriage certificate
- ☐ Mortgage papers
- ☐ Visa/passports
- ☐ Real estate titles/deeds
- ☐ Adoption papers
- ☐ Social Security card
- ☐ Will/Loving Letters
- ☐ Retirement plan/401(K)
- ☐ Trust agreements
- ☐ Employment benefit plan
- ☐ Burial instructions
- ☐ IRA papers
- ☐ Guardianship documents
- ☐ Notes/loan agreements
- ☐ List of special bequests
- ☐ Divorce/separation records
- ☐ Life insurance
- ☐ Cemetery lot titles
- ☐ Health insurance
- ☐ Safe deposit box key location
- ☐ Auto insurance policy
- ☐ Military service records
- ☐ Auto title
- ☐ Annuity contracts
- ☐ House title
- ☐ Advance Directives
- ☐ Tax Records
- ☐ Flood/Property Insurance
- ☐ Income tax records

NAMES OTHERS CHOSE FOR THEIR GOING AWAY BOOK

Approaching the naming of your book with a touch of humor is a reminder that dying is only one part of the life God has given us, and it can be embraced as a part of a process that cannot be avoided. Here are book names others have chosen:

- *19th Hole*
- *Amen*
- *Angel Wings*
- *Bye Bye,*
- *'See You Later*
- *Death Matters*
- *Exodus*
- *–30–*
- *Going, Going, Gone*
- *Hosta La Vista*
- *Last Farewell*
- *My Final Exit*
- *On Eagle Wings*
- *The Final Round*

- *2 Minute Warning (Possible Overtime)*
- *Close the Corral Gate*
- *For My Family. . . Because I Love You*
- *From Here to Eternity*
- *Honeymoon Book 1 (After the Going Away)*
- *On the Road Again and Laughing All the Way*
- *Our Going Away Book*
- *So Long, It's Been Good to Know You*
- *Somewhere in Time (or I Did It My Way)*
- *Somewhere Over the Rainbow*
- *What Did You Do with the Wrapper?*
- *The Last Roundup*
- *Gone Are The Days*

WHAT'S NEXT?

At this point you've got a book name, chapter names, possible sections within each chapter, topical documents within each section heading, and a start towards putting the important documents and forms you want to keep in your book.

Go to the next chapter, "Instant Action." The work you do in the "Instant Action" chapter of your book may be the most important thing you've ever done.

Instant Action on YOUR Death

You need a plan before this happens

A visiting minister prayed, "Dear Lord," he began, with arms extended toward heaven and with a rapturous look on his upturned face, "Without you we are but dust."

He would have continued, but at that moment a very observant daughter (who was listening!) leaned over to her mother and asked quite audibly in her shrill little girl voice, "Mom, what is butt dust?"

AN END OF LIFE STORY

For a quick change of pace, read this little script about your death.

Characters:
>   Narrator
>   Joe
>   Mary
>   Alice

(Narrator) *Your death occurred at home, with the adult children standing by. Hospice didn't have to get involved, even though they had been talked to. All the family is there now; luckily, all the kids live in the same town. You had been going downhill for some time. You weren't in pain; your heart just gave out, just as it had done previously for your partner of 48 years.*

There was some confusion, of course. No one knew what to do next. You had handled all the arrangements for your wife. After the initial shock, somebody thought of Your Going Away book. They knew it was in a big 3-ring binder you kept on the shelf in the Study.

(Joe) "I'm surprised we didn't think of it sooner. Dad certainly talked about it a lot. So much, it was boring."

(Narrator) *They found the book in the study, placed very prominently in sight. On the very first page was the Instant Action form.*

(Mary) *Reading the first page,* "Great, we've got a plan. We didn't have to think it out. Who'll make the calls?"

(Alice) "Dad's family has to be notified first. I see these phone numbers. I'll call them."

(Mary) "I'll use my cell and call the minister, old what's his name. His phone number is on this form."

(Alice) "I see the names of two old friends here; I'll call them, too. They know stuff we don't know. They'll be a big help. I think the last time we talked with Dad about death, we were told these two people were briefed on what to do."

(Joe) "I'll send the emails. We'll get notes to the others tomorrow, or call. The list of those persons who don't get email is not too long. Of course, we'll have to contact them all again with the service information. But with email, it's easy."

(Mary) "Wow, what a relief."

(Alice) "I see Dad listed Dick Jones, one of the two old friends, as a person who can make decisions about picking up the body. 'Wonder what he said to him? Better call him right away."

(Mary) "I was going to call a mortuary, but I see he listed the name of a crematory. Does he want to be cremated? I guess I wasn't paying attention when we discussed this last Christmas."

(Alice) "I just got off the phone with Dick Jones. He wasn't too surprised at Dad's death. Said he knew the 'old grim reaper' was right around the corner. He also confirmed what we thought: cremation. Dick is coming right over. 'Said he'd make the call to the crematory. He told me they would also handle the death certificate, and, since we're moving so fast, there will be no embalming charge."

(Joe) "Somebody put on the coffee pot. I need a few minutes by myself. I wish I had told Dad how much this advance preparation stuff helps."

(Narrator) *This is the end of day one . . . the day you died. What do you think? Are things going about the way you thought they would? Can you imagine the confusion family members would experience if there were not some form of guidance available? What would they have to do? Visualize the stress they would feel at the same time they were mourning your death.*

The story of your death continues... A night has passed and it's now the morning after their Dad's death. The family is sitting around the kitchen table, having a second cup of coffee after a breakfast of the family favorites, poached eggs, bacon, English muffins, and hash browns.

(Alice) "I was looking through Dad's Going Away book at the section called, 'My Going Away Party.' That's the name he chose for his Memorial Service. There is an awfully lot of information in that section. I know things now about the folks I never knew before. It's really pretty amazing. Have you read it?"

(Narrator) *No one had, but all promised to take a look at the book after they'd dressed for the day. The "Book" had been moved to the kitchen since that was the place where they all seemed to congregate.*

(Mary) "I guess the cremation is over by now. Dick certainly handled that efficiently. He said they would probably do it a couple of hours after they got the body and paperwork completed.. He said it was not necessary for us to be there when they did it, but I still feel kinda weird.

"By going the cremation way, we won't be having a visitation at a funeral home. That means we have to think about a Memorial Service. The pastor is coming over in about an hour, so we need to be ready to talk to him. "

(Joe) "One more thing we don't have to worry about is the obituary. It's finished, except for a couple of paragraphs. I found an Obituary Preparation sheet in the book that Dad had filled out and his Obituary Narrative was prepared from that data. There's some pretty creative writing in that obit. Look at how this was prepared ...."

End

MORE QUESTIONS

Are you beginning to see how advance preparation pays off? Let's respond to a few more issues. Below are questions that have to be asked and answered, sooner or later. See if you can answer them all.

- ☐ Are there parts of your life that you want to be sure someone knows about?
- ☐ Do you have stories you want to share?
- ☐ Would your survivors know what minister to notify?
- ☐ Would your survivors know whether you want to be cremated or buried?
- ☐ Where do you want to be buried?
- ☐ What kind of a funeral do you want?
- ☐ Would your survivors know the doctor to call to verify your death?
- ☐ Would your survivors know other persons to notify?
- ☐ What do you want your obituary to say?
- ☐ Where is your will?
- ☐ What do you want done with your household goods?
- ☐ How are your personal possessions to be divided?
- ☐ Does someone else have a key to your strong box and authority to get into it?
- ☐ Does someone know where the emergency funds are that will keep bills paid until your estate is settled?
- ☐ Can someone besides you sign on your checking accounts?
- ☐ Does someone besides you have the authority to dispose of your assets, like stocks and bonds?
- ☐ Have you identified the goals you have for the rest of your life?
- ☐ What do you want done if you cannot make medical or personal decisions for yourself?
- ☐ Are there things you really want to accomplish before you die?

How'd you do? Do you feel like you've got a lot of work to do? Are you ready to "get ready?"

This is a very important chapter. The work you do will tell others what you want done shortly after your death. That's why the chapter is titled "Instant Action." Time is of the essence just after you die. But it's likely things won't move along too quickly because of the anguish, sorrow, tears, questions, fears, confusion, doubt, and all the other emotions dying creates. It's a stressful time. The period immediately following your death is an extremely difficult time to have to make major decisions. Remember the examples from the "Instant Action"form that were in Chapter 1? This is the lifesaver we'll be working on now.

You'll need to start gathering up information about yourself and other members of the family. You'll also have to begin making some tough personal decisions. Luckily, nothing is enclosed in concrete until you die. So, for now, you can change your mind as many times as you wish.

INSTANT ACTION INSTRUCTIONS

Let's get started on your Instant Action form. Answer the questions as best you can. Pencil in the answers below if you want, but in your notebook is a better place.

- [ ] Family members to notify (other persons to be notified are listed on your "People I Want to be Notified of My Death" form; some can be emailed, others called or written to)
- [ ] Minister to call
- [ ] Two close friends to call for support
- [ ] Hospice (if they have been involved)
- [ ] Contact this person who knows what I want done with my body
- [ ] Funeral home or crematory and phone number to call to remove my body (in case of an unusual circumstance like an accident, crime or suicide, the coroner or sheriff's office should first be called)
- [ ] Burial instructions–where more information can be found
- [ ] Doctor to certify death
- [ ] Personal attorney
- [ ] CPA/Financial advisor
- [ ] Life insurance agent

ADDITIONAL HELPFUL INFORMATION
(This data is in addition to your "Instant Action" form, but should not conflict.)
    The information will come in handy many times in the few days after your death. It's important, so go ahead and prepare the responses and file them in your Instant Action section.

- ☐ Give the jewelry on my body for safe keeping to *(name)*
- ☐ Get 12 extra copies of my death certificate from the mortuary/crematory:
- ☐ Life Insurance Information is located
- ☐ Social Security notification
- ☐ Veteran's info
- ☐ Make Memorial Donations of the specified amounts in my will to
- ☐ Send notice of my death to these organizations
- ☐ Obituary information located
- ☐ Place my obituary in these publications
- ☐ Sheriff's phone
- ☐ Coroner's phone
- ☐ Pet care at
- ☐ Provides child care
- ☐ Cleaning service
- ☐ Has authority to pay bills
- ☐ Extra house keys with
- ☐ Nearby places where out-of town guests might stay
- ☐ Utilities/Misc Account Info
    - ☐ Electric ☐ Gas ☐ Garbage
    - ☐ Water ☐ Lawn Service ☐ Security
- ☐ Magazines are on a separate list in my Going Away book
- ☐ Credit Card information
- ☐ Department stores, other accounts

    After you die, you'll want remembrances of your life to be a celebration! But it's got to be a party!
    The checklist that follows will let you express your preferences. Some of your friends undoubtedly died badly because they didn't see death coming and didn't plan accordingly. A person can't know how long they will live, but preparing for your final exit will give you the chance to take charge and make important decisions.

Make sure your survivors know your wishes when that time comes. That means, write them down.

Most of the information in the following list will not be needed at the time of your death, but will be very soon thereafter. You don't need to write the answers right now; you'll see them again later on in another chapter. Just review the list for now.

A REVIEW LIST OF AFTER DEATH EVENTS

- ☐ Inform people of my death *(Lists are included in the "Instant Action" chapter of my Going Away book.)*

I want my body

- ☐ Handled according to my Funeral Plan instructions
- ☐ Buried immediately
- ☐ Given to science
- ☐ Handled by this mortuary
- ☐ Prepared for viewing
- ☐ Buried following a service
- ☐ Buried in a casket described in my Going Away book
- ☐ Buried inside an outer burial container described in my Going Away book
- ☐ Buried in this cemetery
- ☐ Cremated immediately without embalming

I want my ashes

- ☐ Scattered   ☐ Kept in an urn at

My burial clothing

- ☐ If I chose a viewing, I want to wear these clothes
- ☐ I want my body to be made up
- ☐ I want my glasses on my face
- ☐ I want to wear this jewelry
- ☐ I want to wear my fraternal and/or military insignia
- ☐ Before burial, remove my jewelry and insignia and give it to
- ☐ If I have chosen to be cremated, I want to wear these clothes

Viewing

- ☐ I want a viewing and visitation
- ☐ I do not want a viewing and visitation
- ☐ I want an "open" casket at the viewing

☐   I do not want an "open" casket at the viewing
☐   I would like pictures of special events in my life displayed at the viewing. The pictures are located:

My burial/memorial service

☐   I want people to know my religious preference to be
☐   I would like the presiding minister to be
☐   I would like these ministers to assist in the service
☐   I want the scriptures I have specified read at my service *(regardless of the type service)*
☐   I want the emphasis in the service to be on my faith and my devotion to my family and friends
☐   I want the emphasis in the service to be on living a good life
☐   I want a formal funeral service in the church
☐   I want a formal service in a funeral home
☐   I also want a graveside service where those who wish may attend
☐   I also want a graveside service for family only
☐   I ONLY want a graveside service
☐   I want a funeral procession to the grave site
☐   I want an informal service, celebrating my life
☐   I want an unusual service, details of which are described in my Going Away book
☐   I want a memorial service at the church
☐   I want a memorial service at the funeral home
☐   I do not want the casket to be present during the service
☐   I want the open casket displayed during the service
☐   I want a closed casket displayed during the service

Music at my service
I want this type of music:
    ☐ traditional religious   ☐ contemporary religious
    ☐ classical   ☐ country   ☐ modern/jazz
I want the music performed by:
    ☐ soloist   ☐ duet   ☐ choir   ☐ congregational singing
    ☐ jazz band   ☐ string ensemble   ☐ organ
    ☐ bagpipes
☐   I want specific music played/sung *(the titles and other information are filed in my Going Away book)*

Pallbearers

☐ The names, addresses and phone numbers of those I would like to be pallbearers are filed in my Going Away book

☐ The names of those I would like to be HONORARY pallbearers are filed in my Going Away book

Eulogies

☐ I would like eulogies by friends and other persons who wish to speak

Flowers or donations

☐ I would appreciate flowers
☐ My favorite flowers are
☐ I would rather have donations made to

My obituary

My prepared obituary is included in my Going Away book. I want my obituary printed in the following:

☐ Funeral bulletin
☐ Church newsletter
☐ Home town newspapers
☐ Social organization newsletters
☐ High school alumni notice
☐ College alumni notice
☐ Fraternal publication
☐ Business publications
☐ Other
☐ Emailed to the list in my computer address book titled "On My Death"

Guest book, gifts register, etc.

The Guest Signing book, the Record of Gifts and Flowers to be kept by

Special readings or visuals

I want a special reading that is filed in my Going Away book
    ☐ read ☐ Included in the program bulletin

☐ I want slides or videos shown

Statement of my beliefs

☐ I want my statement of beliefs read *(filed in my Going Away book)* and printed in the program

Reception following the service

☐ I do not want a reception after the service
☐ I want a reception after the service
☐ I would like the reception held at
☐ I want something else entirely which is described in my Going Away book.

At the reception, I would like these events to take place

☐ Music   ☐ Entertainment   ☐ Other   ☐ Food

NOTE: You will be actually planning your funeral/memorial service later on.

I told you it would be scary.

There are a million things to do and you won't be around to do them. If your preferences are not written down before you die, someone will do the best they can. My guess is that they will do a very good job, but they'll be under an awfully lot of stress. Can't you can see how your advance work will be helpful?

Think about it.

Make decisions NOW... for When you Can't

The legal documents you need when you need them

One summer evening during a violent thunderstorm, a mother was tucking her son into bed. She was about to turn off the light when he asked, with a tremor in his voice, "Mommy, will you sleep with me tonight?"

The mother smiled and gave him a reassuring hug. "I can't dear," she said. "I have to sleep in Daddy's room."

A long silence was broken at last by his shaky little voice, "The big sissy."

ADVANCE DIRECTIVES

If you are admitted to the hospital, the hospital staff will probably ask you *(or a member of your family if you are incapable of responding)* if you have signed Advance Directives relating to your care. (*What would you say if asked that right now?*)

You routinely hear talk about "Advance Directives." I believe many of us don't know much about them. Right?

This chapter will begin to increase your understanding of the four major Advance Directives. It's not the most exciting prose you'll ever read, but this is not a topic you can ignore. In fact, getting these directives into place should be a priority for you. That's a true statement regardless of your age.

The objective of Advance Directives is to put you in charge of your life... and death. Not a bad idea, huh?

A specific question usually asked on admittance to a hospital is, "Do you have a Medical Power of Attorney for Health Care or a Directive to Physicians and Family or Surrogates?" (*This latter one is also referred to as a "Living Will."*) If you understand the two documents and your answer was, "Yes, I have them," go to the head of the class. If you're scratching your head, stay with me.

There is a lot of information available on personal directives, much of it difficult to read. This chapter cuts through the legal mumbo-jumbo and tries to use words that are easy to understand. If you decide you need technical guidance and specific complicated language, get legal help or try the social services department of a large hospital.

Before we go any further, you **do not have** to create Advance Directives. It's not the law. However, it only makes sense to create your personal directives for two good reasons. One, if you have unique needs, Advance Directives insure everybody knows about them. Two, it is a gracious thing to do for your family. Having your wishes in writing relieves them of having to make gut-wrenching decisions at a time of great stress.

Directives are generally state legislature approved documents. The difference between states is not great, but it's a good idea to use the one your legislative representatives have approved. (*I'm not absolutely positive, but I believe any document you executed would probably be OK. But don't take the chance. Use the one your state suggests.*)

TYPES OF ADVANCE DIRECTIVES

There are four directives that will be emphasized in this chapter:

1. Medical Power of Attorney (*formerly known as a Durable Power of Attorney for Health Care*)
2. Directive to Physicians and Family or Surrogates (*commonly referred to as a "Living Will"*)
3. Out-of-Hospital Do-Not Resuscitate Order
4. Declaration for Mental Health Treatment

Two other directives are of importance but are not covered in this chapter:

5. Appointment of a Guardian for Adult, Minor, or Disabled Children
6. Appointment of an Agent to Control Disposition of Remains

WHAT IS AN ADVANCE DIRECTIVE?

An Advance Directive tells in advance, naturally, how you, as the person signing the document, want a medical or mental situation to be handled or how you want to be treated if you are involved in an accident or are ill. In the context of this book, Advance Directives are documents that state your choices for health care, the kind of treatment you want depending on how sick you are, or name someone to make decisions if you are unable because of illness or injury.

For example, a directive would describe what kind of care you want if you have an illness you are unlikely to recover from, or if you are permanently unconscious (*in a coma, for example*), or the medical care you want if you become unable to make medical decisions.

By putting your wishes in writing before the event occurs, you take the burden to make difficult decisions off your family and doctors. And, by doing so in advance, you will probably pass any legal test as to your state of mind.

Think of it this way: Advance Directives tell your doctor you don't want certain kinds of treatment or that you want a certain treatment no matter how ill you are. Having Advance Directives in place is a demonstration that you care for your loved ones. . . and yourself.

CREATING ADVANCE DIRECTIVES

An Advance Directive can be created using:

- A state-approved form provided by your doctor, a medical facility, or your attorney
- Words you write without regard to form (not the best idea!)
- Your lawyer (if you do this, you might want to consider using an attorney who specializes in Elder Law)
- The services of your State Department of Human Services
- A computer software package for legal documents

KEY FACTS ABOUT ADVANCE DIRECTIVES:

- Advance Directives do not have to be complicated legal documents. They can be short, simple statements about what you want done or not done if you can't speak for yourself.
- Anything you write by yourself or with a computer software package should follow state laws. The original should be filed in your Going Away book. Copies should be given to your agent, family, your doctor, and hospital authorities.
- Advance Directives do not need to be notarized, only witnessed, signed and dated. (However, getting the document notarized is OK if you want to.)
- Two witnesses are required to sign a directive. Only one may be a family member or care-giver.
- Not having Advance Directives will not impact your access to care.
- Having an Advance Directive will not affect insurance policies or premiums.
- Advance Directives executed in another state are valid in most states.
- If one Advance Directive conflicts with another, the later dated document supersedes.
- You can revoke an Advance Directive at any time.

REASONABLE QUESTIONS REGARDING ADVANCE DIRECTIVES

Do i have to have an advance directives?

No. You may not be forced to sign an Advance Directive. You may not be denied medical care or insurance coverage because you choose not to sign one. You are not required to complete Advance Directives as part of patient registration in a hospital, skilled nursing facility, home and community support services agency, personal care facility, or special care living facility. You will probably be asked if you have them.

Most Advance Directives are written for or by older or seriously ill people. For example, someone with terminal cancer might write that she does not want to be put on a respirator if she stops breathing. This action can reduce her suffering, increase her peace of mind, and increase her control over her death.

However, even if you are in good health, you should consider writing Advance Directives. An accident or serious illness can happen suddenly, and if you already have signed directives, compliance with your wishes is more likely,

How do I know my directives will be followed?

Most hospitals are committed to honoring a patient's rights to make his or her own medical decisions, including the right to refuse treatment. Most hospitals have adopted formal policies that acknowledge a patient's right to make an informed decision concerning medical care to the extent permitted by law. In addition, the policies acknowledge a patient's right to have Advance Directives and to honor treatment decisions made by a patient's Medical Power of Attorney form.

What if I don't have an Advance Directive?

If you have not signed an Advance Directive and you become ill and cannot state your wishes, your attending physician and family members can make decisions about your care. You will not know if they are following your wishes.

Where can I get the Advance Directive forms?

Generally, you can get Advance Directive forms in the Pastoral Care and Social Work departments of medical facilities, state agencies, or check on line, or with your doctor, clergy, or attorney.

When should I complete Advance Directives for myself?

It is never too soon to talk about serious illness and what treatments you want if you were too sick or unable to specify the treatment choices. This topic is important for everyone to think about, so talk with your doctor and family, and put your choices in writing. An Advance Directive is your life on your terms. Whether you're 18 or 80, documenting your wishes today means your family won't have to make emotional decisions.

Where should I keep my Advance Directives?

Keep the originals of your Advance Directives that you have signed in your Going Away book. Tell everybody where they are. Give a copy to your regular doctor and others who are likely to be with you if you become seriously ill. Give a copy of your living will and your medical power of attorney to the person you have chosen as your agent. Keep a record of everyone who has a copy in your Going Away book. Consider keeping copies in the glove box of your car.

Remember, you can change or cancel an Advance Directive at any time. If you wish to cancel an Advance Directive while you are in the hospital, tell your doctors, family, health care agent, and others who need to know.

A SHORT DISCUSSION OF DIRECTIVES

MEDICAL POWER OF ATTORNEY

A Medical Power of Attorney allows you to appoint someone *(your "agent")* to make health care decisions for you if you are no longer able to make decisions for yourself. The Medical Power of Attorney applies only to health care decisions. It does not apply to financial matters. The health care decisions include:

- Agreeing to or refusing medical treatment;
- Deciding not to continue medical treatment; or
- Making decisions to stop or not start life-sustaining treatment.

The person you choose as your agent makes decisions for you only if you cannot make decisions for yourself. Your agent may not make decisions regarding:

- Voluntary inpatient mental health services
- Convulsive treatment

- Psychosurgery
- Abortion
- Withholding treatment intended for comfort

Discuss the directive with your agent, your physician, and/or attorney before you sign it. As mentioned, put the original of this directive in your Going Away book where others can easily find it and give your agent, your physician and/or attorney a copy of your signed Medical Power of Attorney form.

You can change or cancel your Medical Power of Attorney at any time for any reason.

DIRECTIVE TO PHYSICIANS AND FAMILY OR SURROGATES (YOUR "LIVING WILL")

This Advance Directive applies only to health care decisions. It does not apply to financial matters. A Directive to Physicians and Family or Surrogates (*Living Will*) is a form that allows you to instruct physicians to administer, withdraw, or withhold life-sustaining treatment when it has been determined by your physician that you have an irreversible or terminal condition and you are not able to communicate your wishes.

Life-sustaining treatment includes life-sustaining medications and artificial life support, such as mechanical breathing machines, kidney dialysis and artificial nutrition and hydration, none of which is expected to cure your condition or make you better, and is only prolonging the moment of death.

Discuss this document with your physician, family, clergy, friends, or your attorney before you sign it.

The original of your Living Will should be placed in your Going Away book and a copy given to your physician, family members or significant others, the person chosen as your agent to make health care decisions and/or your attorney.

You can change or cancel your Living Will at any time for any reason.

OUT-OF-HOSPITAL DO-NOT-RESUSCITATE (DNR) ORDER

An Out-of-Hospital DNR Order is a form completed by an individual and physician that allows the individual to refuse specific life-sustaining treatments outside of a hospital inpatient setting.

Any adult who is capable of making and communicating informed health care decisions can prepare an Out-of-Hospital DNR

Order. **However, to show that you have an Out-of-Hospital DNR Order, you must have the original or a copy of your form with you or wear an approved ID necklace or bracelet. The Out-of-Hospital DNR Order form and bracelet must be obtained through a physician.** Consult with your family physician or legal professional about obtaining or completing the directive. Discuss the document with your physician, family, clergy, and/or friends before you sign it.

You may cancel the Out-of-Hospital DNR Order at any time.

The original of your Out-of-Hospital DNR Order should be placed in your Going Away book and a copy should be given to your physician, family members or significant others, the person chosen as your agent to make health care decisions and/or your attorney. Put a copy in your car's glove box.

DECLARATION FOR MENTAL HEALTH TREATMENT

In the event you become mentally incapacitated, the Declaration for Mental Health Treatment allows you to tell a hospital that provides mental health services what kinds of mental health treatment you do or do not agree to (*including such options as psychoactive medications, convulsive treatment, and preferences for emergency treatment such as restraint, seclusion, or medication*).

Consult a lawyer if you have questions about how the Declaration for Mental Health Treatment works in your state and under what circumstances your decisions can be overridden.

For the Declaration for Mental Health Treatment to become effective, a judge must find that you are incapacitated because you lack:

- The ability to understand the nature and consequences of a proposed treatment, including the benefits, risks and alternatives, and;
- The ability to make health care treatment decisions because of impairment.

The law defines "incapacitated," and the court determines "incapacitation" in one of only two ways:

- In a guardianship proceeding, or
- In a hearing to consider the forced administration of psychoactive medication.

The Declaration form can be obtained from a psychiatrist, psychologist, licensed social worker, other mental health provider, or an attorney. Once signed, the declaration is generally valid for only three years from the date it is signed. Consult your family physician or legal professional for more information.

The original of the signed Declaration for Mental Health Treatment document should be placed in your Going Away book and a copy of the signed document given to your physician, family members or significant others, the person chosen as your agent to make health care decisions and/or your attorney. You may change or cancel your Declaration for Mental Health Treatment at any time as long as you are mentally competent.

Note: Most hospitals do not routinely provide mental health services. However, in accordance with federal law, it is hospital policy to provide written information to all adult inpatients on admission regarding their mental health treatment rights, and the availability of written policies and procedures of the facility about such rights. People who need inpatient mental health services and are presented to a facility that does not provide those services, will be examined to determine whether an emergency medical condition exists. If it does, appropriate stabilizing treatment will be provided and then the patient will be transferred to a facility that provides inpatient mental health services.

STATE LAWS

The statements above were correct at the time of this writing; however, to be on the safe side, consult a professional. Always use state-approved forms. Check with Caring Connections (www.caringinfo.org) or the AARP Foundation (202-434-2118) for more information.

AN ILLUSTRATION OF ADVANCE DIRECTIVE USE

Following are the comments of an adult male. His mother and father had both died at the same time.

"I couldn't sleep. I woke up, went to the bathroom like I always have to do these days, and then, after I had crawled back into bed, my eyes were wide open. So, I got up. Just like I've done all my adult life.

"Except there was nothing to do but sit in a chair and stare out at the lawn. Then I thought about that "Going Away" book Dad put together and how much help it was to us in the hours right after Mom and Dad were killed in that awful accident. It doesn't seem possible that it was just four days ago.

I got it and I've been sitting here for the last couple of hours, fascinated by the stuff he put into it . . . and how much time it took to do all he did.

"There never was any doubt that Mom and Dad really loved us. They wanted their after-death time in our lives to be as happy as the other times we had together. Can you imagine that?

"Death was instantaneous, you know. There was no suffering. But there're documents in this book that tell, almost to the minute, how he wanted to be treated if he were in a situation where he could be kept alive with machines. Or, if the conditions weren't good for recovery—even though life-sustaining equipment could keep the blood flowing and the right amount of fluids working—he included instructions to shut off the equipment. These were the 'Advance Directives' in his book that covered his concerns.

"Gee, I'm glad we didn't have to make any of those decisions. I don't know whether I could have done it or not. He thought of everything."

DEFINITIONS OF IMPORTANT TERMS

"Artificial nutrition and hydration" means the provision of nutrients or fluids by a tube inserted in a vein, under the skin in the subcutaneous tissues, or in the stomach (*gastrointestinal tract*).

"Irreversible condition" means a condition, injury, or illness that may be treated, but is never cured, leaves a person unable to care for or make decisions for the person's own self, and without life-sustaining treatment provided in accordance with the prevailing standard of medical care, is fatal.

Many serious illnesses such as cancer, failure of major organs (*kidney, heart, liver, or lung*), and serious brain disease (*such as Alzheimer's or dementia*) may be considered irreversible early on. There is no cure, but the patient may be kept alive for prolonged periods if the patient receives life-sustaining treatments. Late in the course of the same illness, the disease may be considered terminal when, even with treatment, the patient is expected to die. You may wish to consider which burdens of treatment you would be willing to accept in an effort to achieve a particular outcome. This is a very personal decision that you may wish to discuss with your physician, family, clergy, or other important persons in your life.

WHAT DIRECTIVES DO

DIRECTIVE	WHAT IT DOES	SAMPLE WORDING
Medical Power of Attorney for Health Care	Appoints someone, acting on your behalf, who can request or deny medical care if you become incapacitated	"I name (name the person) as my agent who has authority to make any and all health care decisions in accordance with my wishes when I am no longer capable of making them myself."
Directive to Physicians and Family or Surrogates (Living Will)	Tells medical workers your wishes regarding life-sustaining care	"If I have a disease or illness certified to be a terminal condition by two physicians and the application of life-sustaining procedures would only artificially prolong the moment of my death, I direct that such procedures be withheld or withdrawn and that I be permitted to die naturally."
Out-of-Hospital Do Not Resuscitate Order (DNR)	Instructs emergency medical personnel or other health care professionals to forgo resuscitation attempts	"If I am in a state of medical decline where there is no chance for my recovery, and death is eminent, I request DNR orders to be in place, with no resuscitation procedures to be used."
Declaration for Mental Health Treatment	Agrees to mental health treatment if the court determines the capacity to decide is lacking	"If (name), being an adult of sound mind, willfully and voluntarily make this declaration for mental health treatment if it is determined by a court that my ability to understand the nature and consequence of a proposed treatment is impaired to the extent that I lack the capacity to make mental health treatment decisions."
Appointment of a Guardian for Adult, Minor, or Disabled Children (not discussed)	Names a person to be guardian for your minor or disabled children	"I appoint (name) as a guardian to make decisions, after my death, concerning minor or disabled children."
Appointment of an Agent to Control Disposition of Remains (not discussed)	Names someone to be responsible for making decisions about what to do with your remains after your death	"I name (name the person) as my agent who will have authority, upon my death, to make all decisions with respect to the disposition of my remains, in accordance with my wishes."

"Life-sustaining treatment" means treatment that, based on reasonable medical judgment, sustains the life of a patient and without which the patient will die. The term includes both life sustaining medications and artificial life support such as mechanical breathing machines, kidney dialysis treatment, and artificial hydration and nutrition. The term does not include the administration of pain management medication, the performance of a medical procedure necessary to provide comfort care, or any other medical care provided.

"Terminal condition" means an incurable condition caused by injury, disease, or illness that, according to reasonable medical judgment, will produce death within six months, even with available life-sustaining treatment provided in accordance with the prevailing standard of medical care.

Many serious illnesses may be considered irreversible early in the course of the illness, but they may not be considered terminal until the disease is fairly advanced. In thinking about terminal illness and its treatment, you, again, may wish to consider the relative benefits and burdens of treatment and discuss your wishes with your physician, family, or other important persons in your life.

HOW CAN YOU BE SURE YOUR INSTRUCTIONS WILL BE FOLLOWED?

It's all pretty legal and specific. But what if the person you've given authority to decides to march to the beat of another drum and won't follow your specific instructions? Someone may have to take legal action. But, to be on the safe side, follow these instructions:

- Make a record. Be specific. A "living will" is a good form to use.
- Appoint a health care agent (*and another person as backup*) to be legally responsible for carrying out your wishes. Make sure you use a Durable Power of Attorney for Health Care form to give them legal authority.
- Discuss your plans with family members and others and give them copies of your directives. Make sure they all understand that you made your decisions while you were lucid and in advance of any physical or mental decline.

PREPARING YOUR OWN DIRECTIVES

OK. Time now to decide which of the four directives you'll do first. I suggest you follow the sequence below, but you can do them in any order. **Your choice**.

After you've selected the first directive to work on, set a date to start. You might want to make a schedule like this:

ADVANCED DIRECTIVE	DATE TO START	PLANNED COMPLETION	FORMS FROM
Medical Power of Attorney			
Directive to Physicians and Family or Surrogates			
Out-of-Hospital Do-Not Resuscitate Order			
Declaration for Mental Health Treatment			

Decide where you will get the proper forms for your state. Start by asking the Social Services Department of a hospital near you. If they are of no help, try the state web page. Next, try your state representative. As a last resort, ask your attorney to get them for you. In the meantime, be thinking about whom you want for your agents and whom you will ask to be your signature witnesses.

INSTRUCTIONS TO OTHERS SHOULD I BECOME ILL *(5 WISHES)*

This directive, the **"Five Wishes,"** makes it easier for you to let your doctor, family, and friends know how you want to be treated if you become seriously ill and cannot tell them. Five Wishes is a gift, as is all of your Going Away book, to your family members and friends so that they won't have to guess what you want. It is easy to under-stand and simple to use.

"Five Wishes" is not yet legal in some states. However, the document is so eloquent it is a model for all of us. If you want to use it, check with your legal professional regarding the legality of the directive in your state.

The key to making this directive work right is your decision regarding picking the right person to be your health care agent.

Choose someone who knows you very well and cares about you, and who can make difficult decisions. Sometimes a spouse or family member is not the best choice because they are too emotionally involved with you. Sometimes they are the best choice. You know best.

Make sure your choice is someone who is able to stand up for you so that your wishes are followed. Also, choose someone who is likely to be nearby so that they are ready to help you when you need them. Whether you choose your spouse, family member or friend to be your Health Care Agent, make sure you talk about your wishes with this person and that he or she agrees to respect and follow them.

Your health care agent should be at least 18 years or older *(in some states, 21 years or older)* and should not be:

- Your health care provider, including owner or operator of a health or residential or community care facility serving you
- An employee of your health care provider
- Serving as an agent or proxy for 10 or more people unless he or she is your spouse or close relative

An example of a personalized Five Wishes directive follows. If you want to use the Five Wishes document, please order it from the Five Wishes web-site. *(www.agingwithdignity.org)*

INSTRUCTIONS TO OTHERS SHOULD I BECOME ILL

I, John T. Leslie, born September 3, 1930, in Joplin, Missouri have created this document, (dated, XXXX), to make it easier to let my doctor, family, and friends know how I want to be treated if I become seriously ill and cannot tell them. These instructions supersede any others that I have made. In this paper, I want to tell you my five wishes:

1. The person I want to make health care decisions for me when I cannot
2. The kind of medical treatment I want or do not want
3. How comfortable I want to be
4. How I want people to treat me
5. What I want my loved ones to know

1. The Person I Want to Make Health Care Decisions for Me When I Cannot

If I am no longer able to make my own health care decisions, in this section I name the person I choose to make these choices for me. This person will be my Health Care Agent. This person will make my health care choices if both of the following things happen:

- My attending or treating doctor finds that I am no longer able to make health care choices,
AND
- Another health care professional agrees that this is true.

My Health Care Agent is over 18 years of age and is not:
- My health care provider, nor the owner or operator of a health or residential or community care facility serving me.
- An employee of my health care provider.
- Serving as an agent or proxy for anyone else.

The person I choose as my Health Care Agent is my wife. Her name is Janice M. Leslie.
She resides at: 789 Random Avenue, Houston, Texas 77594. 281-555-5555.

If she
- Is not able or willing to make these choices for me,
- Is divorced or legally separated from me, or
- Has died,

Then these people are my next choices:

a. John T. Leslie II
789 Random Drive
Houston, TX 77594
281-555-5555

c. Douglas R. Leslie
789 Random Lane
Spicewood, TX 77594
512-555-5555

b. Mark J. Leslie
789 Random Circle
Sugarland, TX 77479
281-555-5555

I understand my Health Care Agent will make health care decisions for me when I cannot. I want my Agent to be able to do the following:
- Make choices for me about my medical care or services, like tests, medicine, or surgery. This care or service could be to find out what my health problem is or how to treat it. It can also include care to keep me alive. If the treatment or care has already started, my Health Care Agent can keep it going or have it stopped.
- Interpret any instructions I have given in this form or given in other discussions, according to my Health Care Agent's understanding of my wishes and values.
- Arrange for my admission to a hospital, hospice, or nursing home. My Health Care Agent can hire any kind of health care worker I may need to help me or take care of me. My Agent may also fire a health care worker, if needed.

- Make the final decision to request, take away, or not give medical treatments, including artificially provided food and water, and any other treatments to keep me alive.
- See and approve release of my medical records and personal files. If I need to sign my name to get any of these files, my Health Care Agent can sign for me.
- Move me to another state in order to carry out my wishes. My Health Care Agent can also move me to another state for other reasons.
- Take any legal action needed to carry out my wishes.
- Apply for Medicare, Medicaid, or other programs or insurance benefits for me. My Health Care Agent can see my personal files, like bank records, to find out what is needed to fill out these forms.

If I change my mind about having a Health Care Agent, I will:

- Destroy all copies of this document, OR
- Write the word "Revoked" in large letters across the name of each agent whose authority I want to cancel and sign my name on that page, OR
- Tell someone, such as my doctor or family, that I want to cancel or change my Health Care Agent.

2. The Kind of Medical Treatment I Want or Do Not Want

I believe that my life is precious and I deserve to be treated with dignity. When the time comes that I am very sick and am not able to speak for myself, I want the following wishes and any other instructions I have given to my Health Care Agent, to be respected and followed.

The instructions I am including in this section are to let my family, my doctors and other health care providers, my friends, and all others know the kind of medical treatment I want or don't want.

A. General Instructions

I do not want to be in pain. I want my doctor to give me enough medicine to relieve my pain; even if that means that I will be drowsy or sleep more than I would otherwise. I do not want anything done or omitted by my doctors or nurses with the intention of taking my life. I want to be offered food and fluids by mouth, and kept clean and warm.

B. Meaning of "Life-Support Treatment"

Life-support treatment means to me to be any medical procedure, device, or medication to keep me alive. Life-support treatment includes medical devices put in me to help me breathe; food and water supplied artificially by medical device (tube feeding); cardiopulmonary resuscitation (CPR); major surgery; blood transfusions; dialysis, and antibiotics.

C. If I am close to death

If my doctor and another health care professional both decide that I am likely to die within a short period of time and life-support treatment would only postpone the moment of my death, I do not want life-support treatment. If it has been started, I want it stopped.

If my doctor and another health care professional both decide that I am in a coma from which I am not expected to wake up or recover, and I have brain damage and life-support treatment would only postpone the moment of my death, I do not want life support treatment. If it has been started, I want it stopped.

D. I have permanent and severe brain damage and I am not expected to recover

If my doctor and another health care professional both decide that I have permanent and severe brain damage, (for example, I can open my eyes, but I cannot speak or understand), and I am not expected to recover, and life-support treatment would only postpone the moment of my death, I do not want life-support treatment. If it has been started, I want it stopped.

I want to be treated with dignity near the end of my life as the instructions above are followed. To be treated with dignity means that I would like people to do the things written below when they can be done.

I understand that my family, my doctors and other health care providers, my friends, and others may not be able to do the things, or are not required by law to do these things.

I do not expect my wishes, which are in the sections below, to place new or added legal duties on my doctors or other health care providers. I also do not expect these wishes to excuse my doctor or other health care providers from giving me the proper care asked for by law.

3. How Comfortable I Want to Be

- I do not want to be in pain. I want my doctor to give me enough medicine to relieve my pain; even if that means I will be drowsy or sleep more than I would otherwise.
- If I show signs of depression, nausea, shortness of breath, or hallucinations, I want my caregivers to do whatever they can to help me.
- I wish to have a cool moist cloth put on my head if I have a fever.
- I want my lips and mouth kept moist to stop dryness.
- I wish to be massaged with warm oils as often as I can be.
- I wish to have warm baths often. I wish to be kept fresh and clean at all times.

- I wish to have my favorite music played at times before my time of death.
- I wish to have personal care, like shaving, nail clipping, hair brushing, and teeth brushing, as long as they do not cause me pain or discomfort.

4. My Wish for How I Want People to Treat Me

- I wish to have people with me when possible. I want someone to be with me when it seems that death may come at any time.
- I wish to have my hand held and to be talked to when possible, even if I don't seem to respond to the voice or touch of others.
- I wish to have the members of my church told that I am sick and that I asked them to pray for me and visit me.
- I wish to be cared for with kindness and cheerfulness, not sadness.
- I wish to have pictures of my loved ones in my room, near my bed.
- If I am not able to control my bowel or bladder functions, I wish for my clothes and bed linens to be kept clean, and for them to be changed as soon as they can be if they have been soiled.
- I want to die in my home, if that can be done.

5. What I Want My Loved Ones to Know

- I wish my family members and loved ones to know that I love them. In this regard, I have written a letter to be read after my death before my will is read. I have non-legal, loving things to say to my family
- I wish to be forgiven for the times I have hurt my family, friends, and others.
- I wish to have my family members and friends know that I forgive them for what they may have done to me in my life.
- I wish for my family members and loved ones to know that I do not fear death itself. I think it is not the end, but a new beginning for me.
- I wish for all of my family members to make peace with each other before my death, if they can.
- I wish for my family and friends to think about what I was like before I had a terminal illness. I want them to remember me in this way after my death.
- I wish for my family and friends to look at my dying as a time of personal growth for everyone, including me. This will help me live a meaningful life in my final days.

- I wish for my family and friends to have memories of my life to give them joy, not sorrow.

If anyone asks how I want to be remembered, I have included in my Going Away book things I have thought of that I would appreciate being said about me after my death. My companion knows my funeral wishes and about written instructions that are in my Going Away book.

If there is to be a memorial service for me, I wish for this service to include music and songs chosen by me, my companion, or other members of my family. They know that happy and joyful music means more to me than sad and slow tunes and that the music need not be religious. I prefer to be cremated and, if my companion can handle the stress, to have only a memorial service. Following the service I wish to have an event that represents joy and happiness, and loving concern for those still alive. Dixieland music would please me. Specific instructions are included in my Going Away book.

If my body would benefit science, I wish it to be donated to a medical facility rather than be cremated.

Signing this form

I have signed this document in the presence of two witnesses and they have signed their names in my presence. As a further indication of my state of mind, I have also had this document notarized.

I, John T. Leslie, ask that my family, my doctors and other health care providers, my friends, and all others, follow my wishes as communicated by my Health Care Agent, or as otherwise expressed in this document. If any part of this form cannot be legally followed, I ask that all other parts of this document be followed.

Signature:

789 Random Drive
Houston, TX 77594
281-555-5555
Month, Day, 20XX

Following are the statements of two witnesses who were present at the signing of this document on this date and are a part of this statement:

I declare that the person who signed this document, John T. Leslie, hereafter "person," is personally known to me, that this document was signed in my presence, and John T. Leslie, the document's author, appears to be of sound mind and under no duress, fraud, or undue influence.

I also declare that I am over 19 years of age and am not:

- The individual appointed as agent by this document,
- The person's health care provider, including owner or operator of a health, long-term care, or other residential or community care facility serving the person,
  - An employee of the person's health care provider,
  - Financially responsible for the person's health care,
  - An employee of a life or health insurance provider for the person,
  - Related to the person by blood, marriage, or adoption, and,
  - To the best of my knowledge, a creditor of the person or entitled to any part of his estate under a will or codicil, or by operation of law.

Signature of Witness 1

Address
City, State ZIP
Phone Number

Signature of Witness 2

Address
City, State ZIP
Phone Number

Notarization

STATE OF TEXAS, COUNTY OF HARRIS. On this _____ day of month, 20XX, the said John T, Leslie, personally known to me to be the person named in the foregoing instrument, and the witnesses, respectively, personally appeared before me, a Notary Public, within and for the State of Texas, of HARRIS County, and acknowledged that they freely and voluntarily executed the same for the purposes stated therein.

My Commission Expires:

Phy·si·cians AND Pre·scrip·tions

There sure are a lot of them

Morris, an 82 year-old man, went to the doctor to get a physical. A few days later the doctor saw Morris walking down the street with a gorgeous young lady on his arm.

The doctor said to Morris, "You're really doing great, aren't you?"

Morris replied, "Just doing what you said, Doc, 'Get a hot mamma and be cheerful.'"

The doctor said, "I didn't say that. I said, 'You've got a heart murmur. Be careful.'"

A DISCUSSION WITH YOUR DOCTOR

Don't you wish your doctor answered your questions this way?

Q: Doctor, I've heard that cardiovascular exercise can prolong life. Is this true?

A: Your heart is only good for so many beats, and that's it...don't waste them on exercise. Everything wears out eventually. Speeding up your heart will not make you live longer; that's like saying you can extend the life of your car by driving it faster. Want to live longer? Take a nap.

Q: Should I cut down on meat and eat more fruits and vegetables?

A: You must grasp logistical efficiencies. What does a cow eat? Hay and corn. And what are these? Vegetables. So, a steak is nothing more than an efficient mechanism of delivering vegetables to your system. Need grain? Eat chicken. Beef is also a good source of field grass (green leafy vegetable). And a pork chop can give you 100% of your recommended daily allowance of vegetable products.

Q: Should I reduce my alcohol intake?

A: No, not at all. Wine is made from fruit. Brandy is distilled wine, which means they take the water out of the fruity bit so you get even more of the goodness that way. Beer is also made out of grain. Bottoms up!

Q: What are some of the advantages of participating in a regular exercise program?

A: Can't think of a single one, sorry. My philosophy is: No Pain...Good!

Q: Aren't fried foods bad for you?

A: YOU'RE NOT LISTENING!... Foods are fried these days in vegetable oil. In fact, they're permeated in it. How could getting more vegetables be bad for you?

Q: Is chocolate bad for me?

A: Are you crazy? HELLO! Cocoa beans! Another vegetable! It's the best feel-good food around!

Q: Is swimming good for your figure?

A: If swimming is good for your figure, explain whales to me.

Q: Is getting in shape important for my lifestyle?

A: Hey! 'Round' is a shape!

Well, I hope this has cleared up any misconceptions you may have had about food and diets!

Remember. . . the questions and answers were jokes, not medical advice!

THE MEDICAL SECTION OF YOUR GOING AWAY BOOK

Start your own Medical chapter within your Going Away book. Call it "Physicians and Prescriptions."

It's important to put all your medical documents in some accessible place because you never know when you or someone else will have need of them. The more detail you have, the better. You already know that health events of the past become very important in future illnesses. As we age, some of the bad things that happen to our body and our mind had their beginnings in a previous illness. And those pesky germs have just been laying-in-wait until exactly the right time, and then bingo! You've got a life-threatening problem.

Doing the things written about in this chapter will take care of any spare time you have. It's a big job, so big that it will takes a real commitment to do it. But the information you gather can truly be classified as a "safety net." This is because, if a time ever comes that your medical history information is the key to your survival, you'll have it.

Here are some suggestions of sections you could include in the "Physicians and Prescriptions" chapter of your Going Away book *(there are examples too).*

DOCTORS YOU USE

Down the left hand side of a page list the medical specialties you use for your care. *(Everybody will have a different list of specialties.)* Then to the right of each specialty, write your doctor's name, phone number, and address. *(Also, in the doctor's space, write the names of as many members of the doctor's staff you know. It always helps to be able to call staff members by their names.)* On the last line, write your allergies.

Here's a sample list:

DOCTORS I USE

Speciality	
CARDIOLOGIST	
INTERNIST & PRIMARY CARE	
FAMILY PHYSICIAN–LOCAL (If primary care doctor not available)	
RADIOLOGICAL/PROSTATE	
UROLOGIST	
DERMATOLOGIST	
OPTHALMOLOGIST	
RHEUMATOLOGIST	
ALLERGIST	
ORTHOPEDIC	
SLEEP DISORDERS	
VETERANS ADMINISTRATION (For prescriptions)	
ALLERGIES	

PRESCRIPTIONS YOU TAKE

You need to keep a list of your prescriptions. If you take a lot of pills, having the prescription names and other information written down will help everyone. (*For example, if you're ill and others have to give your medicine to you.*)

Here's how: Start out writing a consecutive number on each prescription bottle and on the cap (*you'll be able to say to friends, "I only take 15 pills a day. How many do you take?" Watch their faces!*)

Then, starting from the top of a lined notebook (*or do it on your computer in a table*), **number** each line. This number represents the number you gave one of your prescriptions. Divide the page by drawing seven lines down the page (*see chart*).

List the numbered **prescription name** on each line in the second column. In the next column, write the **generic name.** In the fourth column, list the **strength** (*10 milligrams, for instance*). In the fifth or sixth column make a check mark for the **time of day** you take the pill (*am or pm*). In the seventh column, write the **number** of pills you take each day. In the last column, write **why** you take the pill (*what condition it works on, like "reflux"*), or the problem the prescription is to help (*like arthritic pain*), or any other notes you think are important.

PRESCRIPTIONS I TAKE

#	BRAND	GENERIC	Str	AM	PM	QTY	HELPS
1	Aspirin		81	√		1	Heart/blood flow
2	Atenolol		25	√	√	2	Blood pressure
3	Ultracet	Tramadol	50	√	√	2	Arthritic pain
4	Clartin	Loratadine	10	√		1	Allergies

Put the lists in your Going Away book, and every other place someone might look if they were in a hurry trying to find information that might save your life.

If you take a lot of pills, you might want to make a schedule like the one below, showing the pill numbers in an "am" or "pm" line. That way you'll be able to count the pills in your daily pillbox and know whether you've got them all.

												TOTAL
AM	1	2	3	4		6		8	9	10		8
PM		2	3		5	6	7			10	11	7

DOCTOR'S VISIT DIARY

Each time you go to the doctor, keep a little history of the visit. Keep things like:

- The doctor's name and the date of the visit
- Visit Notes–a short write-up in words you can understand of why you went to this specific doctor
- The doctor's diagnosis
- Treatment recommendation
- Prescribed medicines
- Test results *(you are entitled to have a copy)* summarized in plain English *(you may have to do this yourself)*
- What the X-rays or MRI's showed
- Other medical reports and records
- At the bottom of the page write the next appointment date.

Also put the appointment date into your computerized appointment scheduler and make a reminder entry a week or so in advance that will make sure you don't schedule two things at the same time.

HERE'S AN EXAMPLE OF A "DOCTORS VISIT DIARY"

> Dr. Joe Smith, Gastroenterologist
> Date of visit September 3, 200X
> Date of this report: September 3, 200X
>
> My weight at the time of this visit: 185 pounds. Back in 2001, I started having really bad indigestion. It got me mostly at night, after I was in bed. It was worse after I ate a meal heavy with fat *(you know, a good T-bone or prime rib)*. Antacids put the fire out, but I was taking so many I'd started looking for some place to buy them wholesale! I thought I might have cancer, so I made an appointment with Dr. Smith.
>
> Dr. Smith checked me over, took some x-rays, did blood work, ran some more tests, and finally got me to have an endoscopic exam.
>
> It wasn't cancer! I had an ulcer! No wonder I hurt. It was a relief to know, because I was really scared.
>
> The doctor started me on antibiotics, saying surgery wasn't indicated at this time. He also prescribed an antiacid to take every day *(for "good measure," he said)*. As of this writing, I haven't had again the old, familiar burning in my stomach. But I think I'll have to be careful of the foods I eat forever. No heavy grease, no high acids. His words as I left his office, "Watch your weight, exercise, lay off fatty foods and come back in six months."
>
> Next appointment: March 16th, 200X, 2:30.

Having your visit diary available for another doctor to look at might help a lot, especially if you're lying on a bed in your local emergency room, unable to talk, but holding your stomach like you'd like to reach into it and pull something out! The story could go like this:

> *A member of your family presents the hospital-on-call doctor with your notes of several visits to Dr. Smith, a gastroenterologist, all because of stomach pains. You had included in your visit diary a telling comment from Dr. Smith from your most recent appointment. You wrote, "He said this ulcer might be a little more serious than he originally thought." Then you continued with your own remark, "At this examination, I've lost 15 pounds (now 170) since my last appointment with Dr. Smith six months ago."*
>
> *The hospital-on-call doctor (Dr. Jones) tells a family member he thinks the history of stomach cancer in your family is a warning that can't be ignored. He wants to do a thorough work up, one that would keep you in the hospital for a couple of days. You try telling him you can't spare the*

*time right now because of a very heavy work schedule, and that you'll get
back to him as soon as things slack off.*

*Dr. Jones (perhaps in consultation with Dr. Smith) takes a look at
your medical records. Your current situation and medical history become
the telling chronicle, of course. Combine the two and the doctor will have
a good start at figuring out what's happening to you. So, when you hear,
"Now or never," you decide to stay a while.*

As mentioned earlier, you should be able to present to someone the names of all the doctors you go to so they'll know whom to
call if they need to. It's a good idea to keep a record for another reason: you might forget.

YOUR MEDICAL TIME LINE

If you don't want to keep a medical diary, consider making a
"Medical Time Line." It looks like this:

DATE	EVENT
9/12/2000	Heart attack. Got to the hospital in enough time that there was no damage to the heart muscle. Dr. Bruce Lachterman is my cardiologist now.
2/2001	Diagnosed with Prostate Cancer by Dr. Stuart Zykorie. Self-referred myself to MDAnderson
4/2001	Completed 42 radiation treatments at MDAnderson under the supervision of Dr. Kuban.
5/29/2007	Had a TGA *(Transient Global Amnesia)*. Had no short term memory for about 8 hours. Doctors could find nothing wrong, and I got my memory back.

When you go to a doctor because of a pain, or some other
problem, and he cures you, you say to yourself, "Well, that's that,"
and you forget about the doctor. But if, a couple of years later, the
same problem comes up, you wonder who you saw the last time you
had this problem? Having available your Doctors Visit Diary or your
Medical Time Line, and the names of doctors you've seen *(your
"Doctors List")* come in mighty handy. It might save your life.

If you can think of anything else that would make treatment of
your illness easier, add it in this Chapter.

Do your best to keep your records up-to-date. If you do, you
may be able to squeeze out a few more years. I hope you can.

GET INVOLVED IN YOUR CARE

If something does go wrong, the best advice is to "take charge of your own care." Do everything you can to insure you will have a safe health care experience.

The Joint Commission on Accreditation of Healthcare Organizations sponsors the "SpeakUp™" program, which urges patients to get involved in their care. They have provided the following tips to patients:

Speak up if you have questions or concerns, and if you don't understand, ask again. It's your body and you have a right to know.

- Your health is too important to worry about being embarrased if you don't understand something that your doctor, nurse or other healthcare professional tells you.

- Don't be afraid to ask about safety. If you're having surgery, for example, ask the doctor to mark the area that is to be operated upon, so that there's no confusion in the operating room.

- Don't be afraid to tell the doctor or nurse if you think you are about to receive the wrong medication.

- Don't hesitate to tell the healthcare professional if you think he or she has you confused with another patient.

Pay attention to the care you are receiving. Make sure you're getting the right treatments and medications by the right healthcare professionals. Don't assume anything.

- Tell your nurse or doctor if something doesn't seem quite right.

- Expect healthcare workers to introduce themselves when they enter your room. If they don't, look for their identification badges. For example, a patient should know the person who's giving him or her medicine or operating their medical equipment. If you are unsure, ask. Notice whether your caregivers have washed their hands. Hand washing is the most important way to prevent the spread of infections. Don't be afraid to gently remind a doctor or nurse to do this. Know what time of day you normally receive a medication, If it doesn't happen, bring this fact to the attention of your doctor or nurse.

- Make sure your nurse or doctor confirms your identity, that is, checks your wristband or asks your name, before he or she administers any medication or treatment.

Educate yourself about your diagnosis, the medical tests you are undergoing, and your treatment plan.

- Ask your doctor about the specialized training and experience that qualifies him or her to treat your illness *(and be sure to ask the same questions of those physicians to whom he or she refers you).*

- Gather information about your condition. Good sources include your doctor, your library, respected websites and support groups.

- Write down important facts your doctor tells you, so that you can look for additional information later. And ask your doctor if he or she has any written information for you to keep. *(Put the notes in your Going Away book.)*

- Thoroughly read all medical forms and make sure you understand them before you sign anything.

Ask a trusted family member or friend to be your advocate.

- Your advocate can ask questions that you may not think of while you are under stress.

- Ask this person to stay with you, even overnight, when you are hospitalized. You will be able to rest more comfortably and your advocate can help to make sure you get the right medications and treatments

- Your advocate can also help remember answers to questions you have asked, and speak up for you if you cannot.

- Make sure this person understands your preferences for care and your wishes concerning resuscitation and life support.

- Review consents for treatment with your advocate before you sign them to make sure you both understand exactly what you are agreeing to. Make sure your advocate understands the type of care you will need when you get home. Your advocate should know what to look for if your condition worsens and whom to call for help.

Know what medications you take and why you take them. Medication errors are the most common health-care mistakes.

- Ask about the purpose of the medication and ask for written information about it, including its brand and generic names. Also, inquire about the side effects of the medication.

- If you do not recognize a medication, verify that it is for you. Ask about oral medications before swallowing, and read the contents of bags of intravenous (IV) fluids. If you're not well enough to do this, ask your advocate to do it.

- If you are given an IV, ask the nurse how long it should take for the liquid to "run out." Tell the nurse if it doesn't seem to be dripping properly *(that it is too fast or too slow)*.
- Whenever you are going to receive a new medication, tell your doctors and nurses about allergies you have, or negative reactions you have had to medications in the past.
- If you are taking multiple medications, ask your doctor or pharmacist if it is safe to take those medications together. This holds true for vitamins, herbal supplements and over-the-counter drugs, too.
- Make sure you can read the handwriting on any prescriptions written by your doctor. If you can't read it, the pharmacist may not be able to either.

Use a hospital, clinic, surgery center, or other type of healthcare organization that has undergone a rigorous on-site evaluation against established, state-of-the-art quality and safety standards, such as that provided by JCAHO.

- Ask about the healthcare organization's experience in treating your type of illness. How frequently do they perform the procedures you need and what specialized care do they provide in helping patients get well?
- If you have more than one hospital or other facility to choose from, ask your doctor which one offers the best care for your condition.
- Before you leave the hospital or other facility, ask about follow-up care and make sure that you understand all of the instructions.
- Go to Quality Check at *www.jcaho.org* to find out whether your hospital or healthcare organization is accredited.

Participate in all decisions about your treatment. You are the center of the healthcare team.

- You and your doctor should agree on exactly what will be done during each step of your care.
- Know who will be taking care of you, how long the treatment will last, and how you should feel.
- Understand that more tests or medications may not always be better. Ask your doctor what a new test or medication is likely to achieve.
- Keep copies of your medical records from previous hospitalizations and share them with your healthcare

team. This will give them a more complete picture of your health history.

- Don't be afraid to seek a second opinion. If you are unsure about the nature of your illness and the best treatment, consult with one or two additional specialists. The more information you have about the options available to you, the more confident you will be in the decisions made.

- Ask to speak with others who have undergone the procedures you are considering. These individuals can help you prepare for the days and weeks ahead. They also can tell you what to expect and what worked best for them as they recovered.

This information was provided by JCAHO. For more information, visit their website at www.jcaho.org.

Pretty good stuff!

Giving it ALL Away

You need a Will before you do

A minister stood in front of the congregation on Sunday morning and announced he was going to do something new and different for the sermon. He told the congregation that after he said a word he wanted them all to sing a verse from a hymn that the word brings to mind.

The minister began, "Cross."

The congregation sang, "The Old Rugged Cross."

"Grace," was next.

The congregation sang, "Amazing Grace."

"Power."

The congregation sang, "Power in the Blood."

"Sex."

Silence... absolute silence... not a word from anyone. They sat in silence while looking back and forth at one another, not knowing what to do.

Then, from the back of the church, an 87-year-old grandmother stood up and started singing, "Precious Memories."

This chapter is about your will. It's about the way you give "it" all away.

The larger your estate, the more complex your will should be. Generally, regardless of the size of your estate, if there is the slightest possibility there could be any conflict over the distribution of your assets, you should have a will. Better yet, regardless of the size of your assets, you should have a will.

Just common sense. (*Depend on more knowledgeable advice than is written here. Don't do your will yourself; use a professional.*)

DON"T HAVE A WILL?

Do you want someone who will:

- Take over your assets?
- Spend your money without regard to your wishes?
- Wastefully send the government extra sums of your hard-earned cash?
- Decide what your children should receive?
- Pay large professional fees for handling your affairs?

If you do, you are among the 70% of Americans who do not have a will and whose estate will be handled by an executor! It's true what they say: "A man who dies without a will has lawyers as heirs."

Everyone should have a will.

Here are some more truisms:

- Every person over 18 should have a will, especially those who are married or have children
- A will is the only way you, rather than the court, can name your executor
- Without a will, the court can determine the custody of minor children
- Without a will, you run the risk of the court distributing your assets without regard for your wishes
- Settling an estate can keep survivors entangled for months sorting out administrative details
- Even with a will, the grieving experience and emotional recovery is complicated
- Without a will, your assets could be eroded and thereby reduce what is left for your heirs

WAYS TO PREPARE A WILL

There are lots of ways to prepare a will, some of them safe, some risky:

- If you don't have your will witnessed...very risky (*foolish is a better word*)
- Write it on a notebook page...risky
- Use a pre-formatted copy from a web page...not as risky, but risky
- Use a computer software package...may be OK
- Use an attorney without lots of will-writing experience... almost OK
- Use an attorney with lots of will-writing experience... probably OK
- Use an attorney with lots of will-writing experience that your friends have used and recommend... the best choice

KEY COMPONENTS OF A WILL
- *Estate*
- *Will*
- *Executor*
- *Probate*
- *Interim Funds*
- *Living Trust*

Following are short explanations of the above terms:

Estate - A person's total property, such as your house, car, IRAs, etc. It also includes your liabilities and obligations, such as home mortgages, contracts, debts, or loan guarantees for others. It is everything you own and everything you owe.

Will - A document that states what you want to happen to your estate after your death.

Executor - A person you name to carry out the instructions in your will. Your Executor will pay your debts and taxes out of your assets and manage your estate until it can be delivered to your heirs. If you don't have a will or an executor, the court takes over. An executor's fee is typically set by law. Settling your estate **can** be very expensive.

Probate - The official proof that your will is genuine. "Probate" also refers to the process of transferring ownership of your assets. In some states, probate is expensive.

Interim Funds - Your monies that are made available to pay bills and survivors' living expenses between the time of your death and the settlement of your estate.

Living Trust - A "Living Trust" is a legal entity that is independent, separate, and self-contained. The trust holds assets you put into it and is managed by someone you appoint. The trustee manages the assets, protects them and, ultimately, distributes them according to instructions you have given.

Trusts are used to keep assets out of probate, for possible tax savings or tax deferment, and for the protection of assets.

Setting up a Living Trust should be done with the help of a professional.

CHOOSING AN ATTORNEY TO HELP PREPARE YOUR WILL

Get attorney recommendations from people you respect, then interview a few from your list. When you're talking on the phone with the attorney you believe will be right for you:

- Ask if the initial interview is free? It should be.
- Find out up front what you will be charged.
- If your estate is complicated, get a specialist who has prepared documents for many people and who has defended his work in court.
- Be up-front about the size and the complexity of your estate.
- Decide before meeting with your attorney how you want to distribute your assets, recognizing the attorney may have some really neat ideas you should consider.
- The attorney should be able to reduce your after-death expenses. Ask how.
- Can you understand what the attorney is saying? If not, get another one.
- Determine whether there can be trust between the two of you. If in doubt, get another one.

GIVING IT AWAY REVIEW

- Commit to preparing a will and updating it.
- Get help in preparing your will; a professional is probably best.

- Prepare your list of assets to be included in your will and decide how to distribute them.
- Apart from your will, write who will receive items that may not have a significant monetary value.
- If possible, give things away before you die, it's less complicated.
- If you do not want problems after your death, discuss your will with family members.
- Talk to family members together *(not separately, it eliminates suspicion)* and give them a general idea of what is in your will.
- Arrange for interim funds to cover expenses before the distribution of your assets.
- Put the will in your Going Away book and copies in some other places known to others. Don't hide your will!

SOME REALLY IMPORTANT FOOTNOTES REGARDING YOUR WILL

Following is an example of instructions that could be given to your attorney for his use in drafting your will. If you don't like these, draft your own. You will save money if you've thought things through and know what you want. The attorney will have comments about your instructions and will probably recommend points of his own. Listen to him. If you feel uncomfortable, get another attorney.

- After my death, if my spouse is still alive, I want everything to go to her.
- If she is dead, I want everything I own to be divided equally between my three sons. This may require some items be sold and the cash distributed. I want my executor to make this decision.
- If any of my sons are dead, I want his share to be equally divided between that son's wife at the time of my death and any children *(from any marriage)* of my son and another woman. *(Children from a wife's previous marriage are not included in this distribution; former wives are also excluded.)*
- If, during distribution, one heir wishes to own something that has substantial value and the other heirs agree, then a reasonable price *(as determined by a professional)* will be set for

the item and the remaining heirs will be given cash for their share, either from the possessor's share of the estate or paid by the possessor personally to them.

- If more than one person wants an item, then cards will be drawn and the highest card will be the possessor. A reasonable price *(as determined by a professional)* will be set for the item and the remaining heirs will be given cash for their share, either from the possessor's share of the estate or paid by the possessor personally to them.

BEQUESTS/LEGACIES

Bequests and legacies are items or sums of money given as gifts upon the death of the donor. The recipients may be specific people or organizations. The most common method of charitable giving is a gift through one's will such as cash, securities, real property or personal property.

Bequests can be for general purposes, or they may be designated for something specific. Care should be taken to include in the wording of the bequest the purpose for which it is intended.

Some types of Bequests/Legacies

General - Goods, or chattels to be left to specific individuals such as "I leave my grandfather's watch to..." and are usually given separately from the residue of your estate. When leaving sums of money, check with your financial planner for the best ways to reduce taxes on your gifts. There are legal ways to leave the beneficiary with lessened liability.

Unrestricted - nothing stated as to what should or should not be done with the bequest.

Endowment - establishes a specific, permanent fund, like a memorial scholarship to a university.

Specific - funds provided for a specific purpose stated by the donor, i.e., the building of a new medical wing.

Contingent -If the intended beneficiary pre-deceases you, the residue of your gift will go to a charity or some other specified thing or individual.

Residual - the residue of your estate can be left to specific beneficiaries *(the residue is everything that remains after any debts, funeral expenses and legacies have been paid).*

Donor - the donation of organs or your entire body to science.
Business - shares in companies can be left to beneficiaries.

Your bequests or legacies are totally personal to your wishes. Just be very specific when leaving bequests. Fully describe your gifts with explanations; be sure to say where they are *(if personal goods or stocks and bonds, etc.)*. If in doubt about what to do, contact a professional.

ALL FINISHED?

When you've finished with your will, you need to record general information about it in your Going Away book. Clearly spell out any special filings with the court or issues that must be settled before the contents of the will are revealed. A page should be prominently placed in your Going Away book that says, at least, these things:

- I have a Will
- I have no Will
- The original, executed copy of my will is filed in my Going Away book
- It is dated
- Any revisions to my will are also filed along with my will in my Going Away book
- The revision is dated
- The attorney who drew my will and his contact info
- Name(s) of Executor(s)
- Name(s) of Trustee(s)
- Name(s) of Guardians of my children
- The witnesses to my will and their addresses
- Other copies of my will are filed

That's it. Here's the best rule: Amateurs don't do wills. Professionals do. Remember the advice from the beginning of this chapter: *The larger your estate, the more complex your will should be. Generally, regardless of the size of your estate, if there is the slightest possibility there could be any conflict over the distribution of your assets, you should have a will. Better yet, regardless of the size of your assets, you should have a will.*

Taking these steps will contribute to your legacy, a subject we'll be discussing in the chapters that follow.

LOVING LETTERS PREVIEW

For now, here's one way to really add to your legacy: consider writing a caring message and explanation that will be read before your will is opened *(call it a "loving letter")*. The letter is the subject of the next chapter, but for now, your legacy of kind words may be more meaningful than money. It may be your greatest gift.

There usually is some ceremony before a will is read. Someone says something or reads something. I advocate the reading of a will be preceded by reading an informal loving letter from the dead person.

To set the stage, what follows is a wonderful example of a letter a mother shared with her children at the time her husband's will was read. The slightly altered letter is from an article in the August 2009 edition of "Keep It Simple," by Anne Roiphe.

I don't know why you said it. I don't know if a shadow had fallen across you, something appalling you saw out of the corner of your eye. I don't know if it was just coincidence or intuition that prompted you, but about a week before you, my seemingly healthy 82-year-old husband, suddenly died, you emerged from the kitchen ready to go to your office, face clean-shaven, eyes shining, smiling shyly, holding the copy of the Anthony Trollope book you were re-reading, and said, "You have made me very happy. You know that you have made me a happy man."

There I stood in my work outfit, blue jeans and a T-shirt. There I stood with my white hair and my wrinkles and the face I was born with, although now much creased by time, and I felt beautiful. I felt beautiful because of his words to me.

We had been married 39 years. We had held hands waiting in hospital corridors while a desperately ill child struggled to breathe and thankfully recovered. We had made financial mistakes together. We had spent hours out in fishing boats.

We had raised the children and then second-guessed our choices. We had stood shoulder to shoulder at graduations and weddings. We were well-worn. I still had made him happy, and I was proud and flushed with the warmth of his words.

I know I looked beautiful that day. Perhaps not to the young man holding his toddler in his arms who rode the elevator with me; perhaps not to the friend I met for lunch, a true believer in Botox; perhaps not to passersby on the street; but I knew it for a certainty. I was beautiful. I don't believe that inner beauty is sufficient in this cruel world. That's the pap one tells a child. I don't believe that positive thinking improves your skin tone or that loving or being loved changes the shape of your nose or restores the thickness and color of hair.

But I do know that there is a way of being beautiful, even as age takes its toll, that has something to do with the spirit filling with joy, something to do with the union with another human being, with the sense of having done well at something enormously important, like making happy a man who has made you happy often enough. And he confirmed it with his words.

Ten days after that morning conversation, we returned from a concert and dinner with friends and walked down our windy block toward our apartment house. Suddenly he stumbled and fell and died within minutes. As I waited for the ambulance, I remembered his words, a beauty potion I will take with me into the rest of my life.

Keep going. It just gets better.

Loving LETTERS

Probably one of the nicest things you'll ever do

Watch your thoughts, for they become words

Watch your words, for they become actions

Watch your actions, for they become habits

Watch your habits, for they become character

Watch your character, for it becomes your legacy

This chapter is about something that may be new to you: loving letters. *("Loving letters" are also known as "Ethical Wills" or "Legacy Letters," "ending note," "love will," "testament," "life letter," or "farewell with love and instructions.")* The loving letters in this chapter are examples that were read to heirs after the death of the letter's author.

I believe your loving letter will have the most impact when it is read at the beginning of a very somber occasion: the reading of your will.

Regardless of the contents of your letter, the primary intent of what you write should always be to express your love.

Whenever an event occurs that reminds us of the fragility of life *(like your death),* we look for ways to preserve our heritage and history. "Loving letters" revive an old Jewish tradition. There is nothing legal about a kind, loving letter; it is a message from the heart. Such a letter can be both a vehicle for self-exploration and a gift to yourself and your loved ones. You leave it to be read when you are gone, before your will is read. You decide how long it will be. But don't make it too long.

WHAT IS A LOVING LETTER?

It is a way to:

- Document *(or record)* and share your values, beliefs, life's lessons, and hopes for survivors.
- Express appreciation of those who significantly shaped or affected your life or brought you special joy, pleasure, happy memories, etc.
- Express love, regrets, apologies, forgiveness, seek reconciliation or resolution of unfinished business. Share your spiritual faith journey—how you arrived at what you believe, and how your life reflects those beliefs
- Tell key parts of the story of your life—who you are, how you lived, who you loved, what you want people to know or understand about you–trying as much as possible to tell your story in your own, recognizable voice
- Articulate your hopes and good wishes for what happens to your survivors *(but it does not include "I hope you suffer" or equivalent words)*

Everyone gets a copy of your letter to take home with them.

The preparation of your letter is an opportunity to talk about forgiveness and love to anyone who will listen to you. It's a great idea. Say it. Write it. Make it a campaign. You can forgive everybody. Do it. Forgive everybody. You can forgive yourself. Do it. Forgive yourself. Write the forgiveness words in the letter. You'll die at peace with everybody. You'll feel better each time you say the words, "I've forgiven everyone, including myself!" and the people who hear your words will be better off...even if they don't know who you are.

Your loving letter is written at a transition point in your family: your death. Your letter candidly assesses your life experiences and values. It records your attempts to make sense of the world and your life. You can remind your loved ones and friends the basis for how you lived your life and how you figured out where your values came from. And you can pass on the life lessons you want to.

Your will disposes of all your earthly goods—what you want your survivors and others to have. Your advance directives spell out the kind of medical care you want and give instructions for when you can no longer care for yourself. If you've completed the equivalent of the **"5 Wishes"** directive, you've spelled out the things that would make you happy should you experience a disabling health event and can't care for yourself and might not be able to express yourself. Your loving letter tells your survivors what you want them to know. It conveys expressions of love, blessings, personal and family stories you treasure. It articulates what you value and want to be remembered for, what you hope your survivors learn from you or what you want your children and grandchildren never to forget.

I believe your loving letter is more important than your financial legacy. We're talking about a letter that reflects the "voice of the heart." Think of it as a love letter to your family. Every loving letter is as unique as the person writing it.

Don't be fooled into thinking that someone someday will care where you attended elementary school, what your favorite color was, when you got your first kiss, or what toys you owned. Nor are they likely to read an entire volume filled with similar details. These kinds of facts, while fun to remember (*and valuable information for what they're worth*), do not reveal your heart or treasured values and will not paint a timeless portrait of who you really are.

To be relevant for generations to come, don't waste the time of others. To be honored and memorialized for who you really are, and to have others appreciate your words, you must be understood. Being relevant and understood are important goals you will want to achieve in your letter. Your loved ones will want to find true meaning in what you write, so use simple, well-chosen words that will unite and resonate on a deeply human level.

Here's a partial list of common themes in more modern loving letters:

- Important personal values and beliefs
- Important spiritual values
- Hopes and blessings for future generations
- Life's lessons
- Love
- Forgiving others and asking for forgiveness

"Will anyone remember me when I'm gone?" It's a question every dying person asks. They will remember you when they read again and again your loving letter, a document as unique and personal as your very own set of fingerprints. It will be your legacy. Your legacy is a way to "live on" after your death.

Although many think of legacies in financial terms, there is also the spiritual/personal legacy that goes beyond material things, e.g., stories, values, hopes, love, wishes, advice, blessings–all things you can write about in your loving letter.

We all want to be remembered. We want our lives to make a difference. Defining your legacy is a rewarding experience, especially during a life transition or when facing challenging life situations. The tragic losses of 9-11-2001 created for many people a special urgency to document their lives.

YOUR LEGACY

What legacy will you leave? Creating your legacy is a rewarding experience that will live on after your death. There are three types of legacies and you can leave them all.

A LEGACY OF RELIGIOUS FAITH

Share with others what God has done in you and for you personally. Much of the faith of all religions is about legacy. Someone gave it to you. You give it to others. Be sure to say something to your grandchildren. You have an opportunity to influence their lives forever.

Don't blow it.

A LEGACY OF GODLY CHARACTER

The integrity of your personal character will make an enduring impact on the people around you. Give them written examples that will help them remember and emulate you.

A LEGACY OF POSSESSION

This legacy is reflected in your will, not your loving letter, but you can comment in your letter on the importance you place on using for good the assets you have given away.

In summary, in your letter you can reminisce about past vacations, sports events, neighborhood happenings, etc. Write anything that makes the letter meaningful and kind and conveys the fact that your survivors should live on knowing you have died in peace, having forgiven yourself, forgiven any past problems or concerns, and full of love for each of them.

Be careful of the tense you use when you write your letter. Past tense is appropriate.

Don't say anything in your letter except loving things. Write how much you've appreciated your family and friends, the ways they've made your life more complete, and other personal things. It's not a time to preach–it's a time for kind words, words that will live on forever.

What you write will be talked about for years and will be your legend within the family. Make it a positive one, one that will make your whole family proud. Be sure to include enough copies. Everyone will want one for their keepsake.

BEFORE THE WILL IS READ: LOVING LETTERS

Your funeral is over. The crowd has gone. All that are left in the house are your children and their families. The small children are watching TV; the older children are sitting on the front porch doing whatever it is that teenagers do. Brothers and sisters, children of the deceased, are sitting around the dining room table. Everyone is waiting for someone to open the will. Anxiety fills the air.

The folder containing the will is on the table. The senior member of the family reluctantly takes charge. He opens the folder and removes its contents. In addition to the legal will, there is another envelope. Written on the outside is "Open first."

He opens the envelope and takes a document out. Unfolding the pages, he glances at the first page, smiles, and relaxes. "He left us a letter. I'll read it out loud."

```
My Dear Family,
    I first wrote this letter in 1999 after a heart
attack caused me to accept the reality that death
was something I had to face sooner than I'd thought.
Luckily for me, modern medicine and the Grace of God
combined and I was given more time. I've been revising
this letter regularly since the first draft. The more
I've thought about our family and relived the great
times we've had together, there just seemed to be more
things to say.
    We've had some wonderful conversations in the last
few years. I want to thank you again for listening to
my stories and for telling me yours. I know you got
bored hearing me talk about 'olden' times, but it was
important (to me, at least) that you have memories of
when I was a young man and of the great times I had
with my Dad and Grandfather. I learned at an early
age and have passed on to you the belief that there's
nothing more important than family. And we've proved
it! We have proved our solidarity as a family many
times.
    Your Mother and I shared a great life together. I
don't worry about you-all looking after her. You love
her, just as she loves you, and you'll want to make
her last days as pleasant as possible.
    Thank you for watching after her.
```

Looking up, he says, "I guess he hadn't revised this letter since Mom died." He started to say something else, but choked up. Then, after a minute, continued reading aloud.

```
    As a family, I like to think we're a little
different than most. We seldom have conflicts. Each of
you goes out of your way to not say anything that would
irritate or disturb the others. We've all learned that
saying nothing mean, unintentional or not, preserves
the peace.
```

```
     Being able to let your hair down and know that
family is around-family that will not let you do
something you'll be sorry about when you wake up
later. Or, if you do something you wished you hadn't,
it's good to know that everyone will laugh about it
the next day...and then forget it. We've had a few
experiences like that over the years, haven't we?
     The legacy we have is that of a loving, caring
family. If I have ever said or done anything hurtful,
I ask now that you forgive me. I died knowing that my
love for you is so great that I can forgive myself for
any mistakes I might have made with you as you were
growing up. Believe me, I've spent many a restless
night wondering if there were things I should have
done that I didn't do.
     Worrying must have helped. You've all turned out
real good. I'm so proud of you and the grandchildren.
```

The letter goes on for another page and a half. As you'll see, **"Loving Letters"** come in many forms. Following are several examples of loving letters written by others. You'll notice each takes a slant that reflects the writer's personality. Anything goes. You don't have to worry about retractions or someone editing your writing. You're free to say anything. Just remember, when your letter is read, you're dead. Don't say things as if you're going to see everybody the next day. Get what I mean?

My advice is to say only things that will make those who read or hear your words feel good. It's your last chance to mend fences and convey your love and concern.

Don't mess it up.

Just be certain you write one.

A **"Loving Letter"** that the writer intended to be read after his death goes in many directions. Each writer has his own agenda, but, buried down within its contents, is the thought, "I love you," "I only want the best for you," "Don't make the mistakes I did," "Reconcile with your brothers and sisters," and, perhaps most important of all, "Please forgive me."

THE AUTHOR'S LETTER

Here is a letter I've written to my sons and their wives. It isn't finished.

You all know I have been an advocate of preparing "loving" letters to a person's survivors. Here's mine. I am writing this letter while your mother and I are both still alive. At this point, I don't know if your mother will precede me in death, so it's possible that she is reading this letter with you.

If she has died, the executor of the estate, John Jr. (chosen because he is the eldest) will be sharing this letter with you. Each of you have your own letter. They all are identical.

Now, with the preliminaries out of the way, let's get started.

Here are my words of wisdom (with not too many words and not in order of importance):

Treasure your family, your relations, and your friends (in some instances the order could be family, friends and relations-you decide-but always family first).

Be nicer and more polite to those you love than anyone else.

Strive for balance in your life.

Don't work too much of the time. (This is not the same as above.)

Spend quality time with your family and loved ones.

Don't make major decisions that affect the two of you without discussion.

Decide how you will kindly resolve conflicting points of view.

Really listen to people when you talk with them.

Always work hard and find pleasure in what you do.

Smile a lot, be yourself.

Consider the consequences of your decisions and actions before you do anything dramatic.

Be responsible, especially for yourself.

Understand and manage your personal finances.

Exercise, sleep, and eat properly.

Hug someone every day.

Have personal and professional goals.

Apply Christian values to everything you do.

Strive to make the world a better place through service to others.

And my comments about the above statements *(in considerably more detail):*

I want to say again what a wonderful wife I've had. Your mother and I have enjoyed our relationship as friends, lovers and companions for a lot of years. I thank God for her and the time we've spent together. I loved Janice with all my heart. She was my world.

You know I believe there is nothing more important than family. I have said for years that a person should be nicer to his family than anyone else. I've never been able to understand how some people would be courteous to a stranger but speak harshly to a family member. We're not that way. Your mother and I said "please" and "thank you" to one another all the time, and I tried to treat her always like the special person she is. I've observed the same kind of consideration in you boys and your companions. One of the ways we show our love for one another is through kindness. I'm glad to know you all share this belief.

Family is there for one another whenever there is a crisis. Who can you turn to that cares more for you than a child, a brother, wife or brother-in law or sister-in-law? No one. We all have friends that care for us, but I don't believe there is another person in the world that is as concerned for you as your family. Don't ever forget that. We're special—at least to one another.

I appreciate so much your concern for each other. It's obvious to me you love one another. It takes a lot of compromises for a family our size to make each other feel comfortable and loved. You have. On the other hand, we're pretty frank in some of the things we say, aren't we? It's a good thing none of us is thin-skinned!

If you're expecting this letter to contain a surprise, forget it. The major statement of this note is that I love you. I want to say it now, free of pain, free of any concerns about the future. My mind is still sharp, so you can tell I am sincere. I love every one of you.

If, for any reason unknown to me I have offended or hurt you, please forgive me. I would never do such a thing intentionally, but I might have done so unknowingly. Life is too short (especially mine!) to let hurt feelings impair relationships).

I believe in service to others. I've tried to practice what I preach. After I retired I was able to spend a lot of time doing for others. Doing so gave me great pleasure. I would encourage you to find an activity that you enjoy and then find a service organization who provides that same kind of service to those less fortunate. Though I believe a church is a great place for service, there are lots of others. Within the Presbyterian Church I've been able to help as an adult teacher, as a member of the session, as a project leader, as an advisor, as a lay pastor, and as a program developer. I'm proud of everything I did. But, over the years I've also found joy in working at NAM, as a Silver-Haired Legislator, with CanCare, with Presbyterian Outreach to Patients, as a lay pastor, as a member of the Cypress Creek Community Organization, political action groups, Big Brothers, and Crisis Counseling. The experiences I've had also enabled me to be a leader in some of these groups and a member of various boards of directors.

I watched as my mother and father aged and became dependent on others for many tasks. As you know, my father died following surgery at the Mayo Clinic. I talked with him the day before he died (we lived in Chicago at that time). He knew then his time was limited, but he was independent his whole life. I've tried to be independent all my life, too. If that wasn't the case in my last days, to those of you who shared in my care, thank you.

I've since learned from my "Preparing for the End of Life" seminars that there is a sequence of events in the dying process. I look back and recognize them in both my dad's and my brother Bob's lives. As I write this letter, I also recognize some of those events ocurring in my own life. I don't fear death, only I would like to avoid a lot of pain. Hopefully, that was the case in my death.

The conclusion to this letter hasn't been written.

A WORLD WAR II VETERAN *(written when he was in his 70's)*

```
I leave my children the wish that they have:
Decency.
Sympathy.
Empathy.
A sense of Justice.
A respect for nature.
Outrage at man's inhumanity to man.
Assurance of the equality of all people.
Strength to oppose tyranny.
Belief that every life is invaluable.
Insight that those more blessed will share.
Tolerance for all.
Contentment in their being.
Joy in life.
Pride in each other and family.

All love,
Dad
```

MICHAEL'S LETTER

Having disposed of my property through duly executed documents, I now turn to the harder job of leaving to my children, Lisa and David, a set of principles that they should consider in living their own lives and in helping to shape the lives of their children. Here they are:

Do the right thing-as often as you can.

Only worry about those things that you can do something about.

Try as hard as you can, and, having done so, don't look back if things don't work out.

Work hard, but stop before you mindlessly begin work to ask whether you have found the most efficient thing to work hard at.

You are not the center of the universe. If it takes religion to make you realize that, then embrace religion.

Happiness is NOT what feels good at the moment. You also have to consider the long-term consequences of your actions.

Be positive; try to find the best in a bad situation.

Be interested in a lot of things. People who are interested are interesting.

Show everyone you love that you love him or her,
and be sure to tell him or her as well.

Divide the world into two groups: those that are
trying to hurt you and those that aren't. Fight the
first group as hard as you can and cut the second
group as much slack as you can.

In making decisions, tend toward those that
maximize your options.

Procrastinating over a decision until there is no
decision to be made is itself a decision.

The best trait, in a friend, co-worker, or
yourself, is dependability. The second is loyalty.

If you find a good, true friend, hold on to him or
her as hard as you can.

Ask not what people do, but how well they do it.

Be fruitful and multiply.

When things are going REALLY wrong, remember that
which doesn't kill you makes you stronger.

Love like you've never been hurt before, and
dance like no one's watching.

A 90-YEAR-OLD MAN'S LETTER

Money is a curse and the source of most evil.
Therefore I do not want to be guilty of leaving too
much of this evil. Instead, I want to leave you some
good advice which, if you follow it, will bring you
better returns in the Hereafter.

Eternal Happiness

Look for real happiness on this earth. Earthly
pleasures are only for the moment. Real happiness
must be lasting. The Soul will never be satisfied
until it gets back to its Maker. Some happiness can
be enjoyed when you realize that you have received
Sanctifying Grace and have no mortal sins on your
soul. More happiness can be attained when you accept
all your trials, sickness, poverty, and family
disputes as crosses sent for you to bear.

To nobody is sent more crosses than he can bear
because there is always enough grace sent to bear
them if you ask for it. If you bear all your crosses
willingly and can even ask our Lord for more to bear,
you have then derived a sense of happiness to which
the best pleasures of this world cannot compare.
Always bear your troubles willingly. Be good; do

good. Then you will always have peace and be on the right road to heaven.

We always forget we are on trial on this earth. We were made to know God, to love God, and to try to get back to Him in heaven.

Much unhappiness is caused by family disputes. In a dispute, as soon as you notice you are not getting anywhere, you need not give up your point of view providing you are sure you are right, but you must stop arguing - shut up. Do this and you will be surprised how much quicker your argument is settled. It generally settles itself.

I have always considered a man very smart if he has provided for his old age, but I would consider him a lot smarter if he has taken out good insurance for the Hereafter. To receive daily Communion is the best insurance for your eternal salvation.

Prayers and Distractions

Prayer is a conversation with God. Therefore, you must think of what you are saying while you are praying. You can say your best prayers when you are alone. The biggest cause of distraction is your eyes. That's why I would recommend the front pews of your Church. In the back rows you can see everybody and your eyes are not on the Lord.

Picture your Lord as standing before you and you can talk to him as one dear to you. Prayer should come from the heart. An original prayer from the heart is better than any prayer that you know by heart. It is also better than most prayers from prayer books.

Remember, if you asked your banker for a loan, you would not read your request to him from a book. If your lawyer makes a plea to the jury, he would not read it to them from paper. When you propose to your best girl, you do not read it to her from a book. Speed is a handicap to prayer and leads to distraction. Take plenty of time when you pray.

Our Lord is not satisfied with our meaningless mumble when we do not think about what we are saying. We must be either hot or cold or He will spit us out of his mouth. Many a person, when he comes to the end of his life, has shouted, "Oh, if only I had known." It is up to us therefore, to pray for understanding so that we are able to judge what is right and wrong for our salvation.

Love Of God

Thou shalt love the Lord thy God with thy whole
heart, thy whole mind, thy whole soul, and thy neighbor
as thyself. To be at peace with God is to love him
above all things.

You are at peace with God when you are ready to die
any time, especially when you can say, "Rather today
than tomorrow." We do not love God above all things
when we forget him in our madness. A person who
complains and cannot reconcile himself to God's will
shows a lack of faith.

I have always maintained that crying at a funeral
is sadly out of place. It shows a lack of faith in
God. Crying at a funeral does not help anything except
to relieve your body. God knows what is best for us-
He does what is best for us. Then what are we crying
for? There is one thing that most parents and teachers
forget to impress upon their children, and it is that
you must love God more than your mother and even more
than your sweetheart. This is most important but sadly
neglected.

Faith

There is one question which is rarely talked about,
seldom discussed. Why are we on earth? Why did God make
you? God made you to know him, to love him and to get
back to him in Heaven. God has placed us here on trial,
and if we can win out on this test, then we have made
it. God has created us with a free will, which we can
exercise for good or evil.

Even the Devil with all his power cannot make us
commit a sin if we use strong will and a determination
not to do it. But without God's help we are unable
to make it. So it is up to us to pray for grace and
enlightenment. For our Lord said, "watch and pray, so
that you may not fall into temptations." Temptation is
necessary to see if we can stand the test. God never
permits Temptation above our strength to resist.

Charity

It is always better to give than to receive.
Charity should begin at home. A person might send all
his money to foreign missions and yet be unable to
see the daily need all around him. Charity does not
necessarily mean financial assistance. Good charity
also includes a pleasant smile and a good disposition

at all times and a desire to do a good deed whenever you get the opportunity. Try and do at least one good deed each day, but let not your left hand know what your right hand is doing.

I know a good old lady, mother of six children, who always has a pleasant smile for everybody, never says a bad word about anybody. She does not have any money to spend, and if she did, it would first go to her children and the needs of others before she would think of herself, Surely this is charity of the heart, which is better than the giving of riches.

Common Sense

We were put on this earth, on trial to try and win Heaven. That means our main efforts must be for spiritual things and less for worldly gain. This also applies to the education of children. Never let your heart get attached to accumulating wealth; God has given you everything you have to be used for your own salvation and you must some day give an account of it.

Never envy people for their ease and comfort of life. For those who have it nice in this world cannot have the same in the next. The road to heaven is not an easy one. It is destined for man to die but once. And after death the judgment.

Quo Vadis — Where Art Thou Going

It is a good and wholesome thought to think about your death occasionally. I really think that a person who thinks about his death at least once a day would be unable to commit a mortal sin. The ambition of the soul is to be united with God. We are all going to die once and only once. If we could live our life over again there would be no use for any commandments the second time.

The old maxim, "If I could live my life over again I would soon be rich," fades away at your deathbed when the only reason you would live life over again would be to advance your salvation. So why gamble the first time when there is no second time? Try and live your life as you would if you were living it a second time and you will derive a sense of happiness which cannot be compared to the pleasures you now get out of life.

Everybody should be glad to be on this earth and have a chance to attain the great happiness in Heaven. This life is only a preparation for the next. See that you make it. All the pleasures of this world seem as nothing when you arrive at death's door.

AN ENVIRONMENT-CONCERNED FATHER'S LETTER

Dear Kids,

Today, I'm writing my own legacy letter. On this day before Earth Day 2008, I want to share with you some of my wishes for your futures.

For me, Earth Day is a time of reflection, a chance to look back at what we've learned about our fragile ecosystem since the first Earth Day in 1970 and how we've done in the years since in making our planet more hospitable for all of its creatures. Since our very existence is intimately intertwined with our stewardship of Earth, I'm hoping your generation and those that follow will manage our planet's resources better than mine has.

Frankly, I don't remember much about that first Earth Day on April 22, 1970. Your mother and I had been married less than three weeks, I was reporting to my first regular duty station in the Air Force and we were struggling to figure out how we could manage to live in Northern California on a second lieutenant's salary. Although we were relocating to a hotbed of environmental activism, our contribution at the time was pretty much limited to not buying colored toilet paper.

As a family, we've grown to be more responsible over the past 38 years. But even with our relatively modest lifestyle, we would need more than one Earth if everyone lived as we do. And, as more people worldwide attempt to do just that, the strain is showing.

It is cruelly ironic that U.S. oil production peaked in the same year that Earth Day was born. Up to that point, the United States was the world's leading oil producer and exporter. In 1970, 93 percent of the world's energy came from fossil fuels. Although that percentage has dropped to 85 percent today (due mostly to increased use of nuclear power), the world consumes nearly twice as much fossil fuel-based energy than it did in 1970.

Given that fossil fuels are a finite resource in increasing demand and that their carbon dioxide emissions are responsible for many of the world's environmental problems, it is clear that there is trouble ahead.

Considering, too, that the modern global economy was built on cheap oil, international manufacturers that raced to the bottom line in the "boom years," may find themselves foundering as a new world economy emerges. Despite the obvious, there are some who still view the cost of fuel as the problem rather than a symptom of a far greater problem.

The 20 million Americans who took to the streets in 1970 got the attention of federal politicians who went on to pass the Clean Air Act and form the Environmental Protection Agency. But government action has been slow and erratic, falling well behind the relentless pace of change of natural forces.

I'm proud with how each of you has positioned yourself for the challenges that lie ahead. You're all sensible, responsible, productive members of your communities. I believe that no matter what awaits you, you'll come up with creative, thoughtful solutions.

I regret that my generation hasn't done a better job of managing the precious resources of our planet. Certainly our parents did their part, surviving the Great Depression and turning back the tyrants that threatened global stability in World War II. The world our parents turned over to us was one full of promise and hope. And, although we lived many years with the fear of world nuclear annihilation just the push of a button away, those same years were prosperous ones.

Our parents simply wanted us to have what they didn't have. We took it and wanted more. And more, and more. As probably the most pampered generation in history, I think we unwittingly created a culture of entitlement where a man's worth is measured more by what he owns than by his personal code of conduct.

When songstress Joni Mitchell wrote that "we are stardust," her lyrical expression was an accurate reflection of scientific fact. Everything around us is derived from materials that were on this planet millions of years before humans. The genius of man is that he has been able to take the raw materials provided by nature and transform them into the buildings, roads and iPods that we use today. Even the cheap oil that has sustained us for the last 100 years or so is the result of decaying organic matter.

So here is what I hope for you, my children, and your descendants:

Clean air to keep your lungs clear and your spirits buoyant.

Fresh water to drink, bathe and play in.

Nutritious and readily available food to sustain you.

A reasonably healthy life, uncluttered by the ravages of disease, toxins and warfare.

A life partner with which to share the joys and sorrows that will inevitably come your way.

Comfortable shelter to protect you from the elements, to give you safety and refuge in times of stress, and a place where you may rest your body or enjoy the companionship of others.

Friends that will support you in times of need and give you a swift kick in the rear when needed.

Close and cordial relationships with your immediate family members, whose aggregate knowledge reflects the wisdom of generations past.

The confidence that your own life experience has positioned you to make appropriate decisions concerning your own family's welfare.

Proper standing in your own community, commensurate with your skills, knowledge and personal beliefs.

A strong spiritual faith that connects you to your natural environment and keeps you centered on those things in your life that truly matter to you.

That you develop and practice the virtues of compassion, truthfulness and generosity.

That you find contentment in all you do, that you find it within yourself to accomplish your dreams and that you concentrate on matters within your control and accept what you cannot.

That you live a full life, true to your own beliefs without doing harm to others.

With love always,

Dad

A SINGLE FATHER'S LETTER

I missed my calling. I should have been a teacher. There are several things I "shoulda" taught. One of them is what I call "life lessons;" not because my kids (or any one else's) need them but because I have gotten virtually every one of them wrong. I desperately want to insure that others (my daughter and grand-children in particular) avoid the hurt I suffered from not having done so.

In any event you and your brother were reluctant recipients of this accumulated wisdom. ("Oh Pop!") But as you matured you learned to abide my "little idiosyncrasies"—see "rule" 10 in the Will. I had collected most of these sayings into my Ethical Will, but I was reluctant to do anything with them until, on September 18, 1998, my 29-year old son, David, died. Writing about and to David helped the grieving process, and I determined to post the Will on the site his friends had put together in his honor. He doesn't need it now--he's in heaven.

By the way, I wrote the Will not only for David but also for Lisa, my absolutely wonderful daughter who I love with all my heart. (The hardest thing about David's death was to convince you, Lisa, that I would have grieved just as heavily if you had died.) Ever the good daughter, you gave your approval to my posting the Will and disseminating it more broadly.

On Rosh Hashanah, our Rabbi talked about documents embodying the "life lessons you want to pass on to your kids." I had written such a document but had never gotten around to passing it on to David before he died. It finally occurred to me that David is not only in Heaven, but is monitoring this web site. So here it is, David. Whenever you read it I know it will bring a smile to your face and an "Oh Pop" to your lips.

NOTE: Many of these examples were obtained from the internet.

In·ter·ven·tion

Sometimes it really helps

Celibacy can be a choice in life, or a condition imposed by circumstances.

While attending a Marriage Weekend, Walter and his wife, Ann, listened to the instructor declare, "It is essential that husbands and wives know the things that are important to each other."

He then addressed the men, "Can you name and describe your wife's favorite flower?"

Walter leaned over, touched Ann's arm gently, and whispered, "Gold Medal All-Purpose, isn't it?"

And thus began Walter's life of celibacy.

Although use of the term, "intervention," typically creates images of a direct, unexpected, confrontational meeting to address a major problem, modern therapy increasingly uses an "invitational" intervention concept. That is the technique described in this chapter.

The invitational, indirect approach relies heavily on family participation in the process, including the person with an identified issue. The desirable conclusion could be that all family members agree to make desired behavioral changes. The element of surprise may exist, as it does in direct intervention. However, there is no contentious confrontation, and thus the event becomes a loving and caring display of concern.

For seniors, invitational intervention seems to be a good approach. The senior sets the parameters and the signal that will indicate something has happened that requires intervention. Then when others recognize the signal that a change should occur, they can advise the senior and the process moves forward with dignity and respect. It is most helpful when the whole family is involved in the curative process.

The intervention described in this chapter is a leap forward in the process, in that the individual who may require assistance acknowledges that intervention–help–may be required in the future and suggests to the family a methodology to identify the danger signals. In fact, the senior family member may anticipate the require-ment for help long before other family members. The recognition announcement from the family that they, too, see the problem emerg-ing, provides for a plan of action to be quickly implemented.

There may be a time when you become disoriented or inca-pacitated, unable to care for yourself.

Harsh words. You could call it "stress," "dementia," "Alzheimer's," "mind on vacation," "senior moments," or any other phrase that says, "something has changed in my head. And maybe with the way my body works, too."

It's not uncommon for older folks' minds to change. Staying "sharp" is often not a question of exercising your brain, but nature deciding to weaken the flow of blood to your brain or to cause one of many other things to happen that change the way you function.

Do you know it's happening? Some say they do. To others it's a complete surprise. You just wake up one morning and the gears in your head don't mesh. Sometimes there's medicine that makes things work better or delays the serious effects. It's all a part of aging.

If you think something like this might happen to you, consider intervention.

It's a kind and gracious gesture towards your family *(and, perhaps, others who would be responsible for your care)*. Give them "permission" to intervene in your life by expressing to you their concerns about your behavior or health. The intent of the intervention is to catch you before you go off the deep end.

A good time for you to send an "Intervention" letter to your family is right after you have executed the Advance Directives documents. If possible, give them your letter and, at the same time, share with them the formal "Advance Directives." A family discussion will clear the air and make the intervention process, if it ever kicks in, a little easier (but not much easier). In another chapter, this intervention letter is referred to as a "no burden" letter.

Here's an example of how the intervention process could begin *(in this invitational intervention you authorize its initiation; in other instances, the initiation process letter could be written by others).*

```
Dear Family,
As we have discussed from time-to-time, we have
witnessed in either our friends or family members
behavior that seemed to indicate the need for personal
safeguards.
    This may happen to me.
    Accordingly, I hereby agree that if any 3 of you
(that includes wives and husbands, but not children)
send me a note and confirm to me in person your
concerns, I will address the issues you identify.
    Of course, if I'm absolutely bonkers, I'll proba-
bly ignore the whole thing. Then someone else will
have to take action when I am unable to recognize the
need. In that case, exercise one of the appropriate
Advance Directives.

Lovingly,

Dad
```

Well, that's straightforward. Your kids will certainly appreciate knowing that if you start doing strange things there is something they can do before they have to get "legal."

Here's the letter style one family used to notify their father his behavior was becoming "unusual." *(You'll see an actual letter in Chapter 11.)*

Dear Dad,

As you will remember, you asked us to notify you if we observed any changes in you that worried us. We have recently noticed a few quirks—little changes in your behavior that concern us. We view as a problem with potentially serious implications your actions of late, specifically: (The actions of concern are listed).

We recommend the following steps in detecting, diagnosing, or remedying what we have come to view as a problem with potentially serious implications: (specific actions are them listed).

On this date, the three of us sign this letter in love.

What happens next is not predictable. Hopefully, a discussion will result in seeking professional help. If it doesn't, as the father said, there are the Advance Directives to draw on. Of the various directives authorized by a state, the first choice would be using the Medical Power of Attorney; a second would be a Declaration for Mental Health Treatment. Using the provisions of the Mental Health directive is a last gasp option, so be really careful. Use a professional.

Just to make sure you can find some humor in this whole process, here's a neat little twist on the Intervention Letter:

Dear Family,

I, your father, being of sound mind and body at this point in time, recognize that I might start acting strangely sometime in the future (I mean I would be more eccentric than I am now!).

When you become aware of my "strangeness," try first those things that can be done without resorting to attorneys or pinhead politicians who couldn't pass ninth-grade biology if their lives depended on it, or doctors interested in running up the medical bills.

Please try the "let's cooperate" method first.

Try to develop some kind of test. An indication that something is wrong with me is that, after a reasonable amount of time passes, I fail to ask for at least one of the following:

Bloody Mary
Scotch on the Rocks
Martini
Vodka and Tonic
Steak
The Remote Control
Bowl of ice cream
Chocolate
The Business Section of the paper or the funnies.

If I don't pass the test, I need help.

If you can communicate with me, please tell me I've got a problem you are going to work on and see what I have to say about it. I'll do my best to be reasonable and rational. Don't ask for any help from the courts or the legislature. I am acutely aware that the legislative and executive branches of state government are fond of meddling in family matters, and have little concern for the privacy and dignity of individuals.

As I mentioned above, please try the "let's cooperate" method first.

All my love,

And here's another humorous Intervention Letter:

I, (fill in your name), being of sound mind and body, unequivocally declare that in the event of a catastrophic injury, I do not wish to be kept alive indefinitely by artificial means.

I hereby instruct my loved ones and relatives to remove all life-support systems once it has been determined that my brain is no longer functioning in a cognizant realm. However, that judgment should be made only after thorough consultation with medical experts; i.e., individuals who actually have been trained, educated, and certified as doctors.

Under no circumstances–and I can't state this too strongly–should my fate be put in the hands of peckerwood politicians. Furthermore, it is my firm hope that, when the time comes, any discussion about terminating my medical treatment should remain private and confidential.

Living in this state, however, I am acutely aware that the legislative and executive branches of state government are fond of meddling in family matters, and have little concern for the privacy and dignity of individuals.

Therefore, I wish to make my views on this subject as clear and unambiguous as possible. Recognizing that some politicians seem cerebrally challenged themselves (and with no medical excuse), I'll try to keep this simple and to the point:

1. While remaining sensitive to the feelings of loved ones who might cling to hope for my recovery, let me state that if a reasonable amount of time passes-say, two months-and I fail to sit up and ask for a cold beer, it should be presumed that I won't ever get better. When such a determination is reached, I hereby instruct my spouse, children and attending physicians to pull the plug, reel in the tubes and call it a day.

2. Under no circumstances shall the members of the Legislature enact a special law to keep me on life-support machinery. It is my wish that these boneheads mind their own damn business, and pay attention instead to the health, education, and future of the millions of citizens of this fine state who aren't in a permanent coma.

3. Under no circumstances shall the governor butt into this case and order my doctors to put a feeding tube down my throat. I don't care how many fundamentalist votes he's trying to scrounge for his brother, it is my wish that he play politics with someone else's life and leave me to die in peace.

4. I couldn't care less if a hundred religious zealots send emails to legislators in which they pretend to care about me. I don't know these people, and I certainly haven't authorized them to preach and crusade on my behalf. They should mind their own business, too.

5. It is my heartfelt wish to expire quietly and without a public spectacle. This is obviously impossible once elected officials become involved. So, while recognizing the wrenching emotions that attend the period of the prolonged death of a loved one, I hereby instruct my relatives to settle all disagreements about

my care in private or in the courts, as provided by law. If any of my family goes against my wishes and turns my case into a political cause, I hereby promise to come back from the grave and make his or her existence a living (you know what!).

Finally, of the many things that can happen to you, there's this to say about your memory slipping a little: at least you can hide your own Easter eggs!

It's all About YOU...

Family Trees, Major Life Events and Other Personal Matters

Last night, my wife and I were sitting in the living room discussing our aches and complaints.

I said to her, "I never want to live in a vegetative state, dependent on some machine and fluids from a bottle. If that ever happens, just pull the plug."

She got up, unplugged the TV and threw out my beer.

This chapter discusses these topics:
- Your family tree *(the genealogy of your family)*
- Your family's birth dates
- Major events in your life
- Your personal time line
- Your medical time line
- Your employment record
- Your military career
- Your volunteer/service contributions
- Your professional contributions
- Your faith journey *(your belief system)*
- Pictures, DVD's, CD's, and movies

As you can see, it's a very personal chapter.

This is probably the first time you will ever pull this much information about yourself into one place. *(Don't forget: it should be as accurate as you can make it, but if there's a date or two that you don't remember, don't worry about it too much. Just keep going; the information may turn up later and you can always revise your work.)* However, pulling all this data together is a big job and will take a lot of work...and time.

As you start this chapter's assignments, be prepared for those younger to show little interest in what you're doing. Many people have told me their children thought putting names and birth dates in a meaningful pattern was "dull." The really interesting thing is that when your kids hit 50 or 60, they suddenly have a great interest in sharing with their children their heritage and they'll want a copy of everything you've put together. Doing genealogical research is one of the most popular hobbies. *(Care to guess what the largest hobby group in the U.S. is? Playing a band instrument.)*

Let's get started.

YOUR FAMILY TREE

Have you recorded the birth dates, the place where they were born, their current address, and, if they are dead, the date of their death and the city where they died, of your:

- Parents?
- Siblings?
- Grandparents?
- Aunts, uncles, and cousins?
- Your children and their companions?
- Your children's children and their companions?

If you have, you can start making your family's family tree. Most of us have information about our relatives scattered all over the place. For some reason, we can never find it when we need it; as a result, we duplicate data. Then, when we try to put it all together, there are little differences *(sometimes BIG differences)*, and we have to spend precious time sorting things out.

As you start putting your family tree together, you will discover there are pieces of information missing from the various sections. Just keep going. Don't get hung up on one item. You'll get it later.

As you create your family tree, you will, additionally, be creating a centralized record of family and personal information. Put it all in *(where else?)* your Going Away book.

The listing of information about a family begins with marriage and goes forward. *(Although birth dates are very important, two people have to marry to start a family tree.)* Most of us initially start our genealogy with grandparents or great grandparents. If genealogical research turns you on, you can go backward to the very beginning *(you know: when fig leaves were very popular items of clothing!)*. Who knows, there might be a king or a prince back there some place. Or, perhaps, a knight or a highway bandit.

Following is an example of a family tree. My family tree is not the best example in the world. You'll notice lots of incomplete information. I started working on this project in 1992, lost interest and haven't got back to it. *(I hope you appreciate knowing this; I think it represents reality.)*

JASON THEODORE LESLIE
and **SARAH ANN PARSONS LESLIE**
Jason Theodore Leslie
(about 1869 to 4/14/1903)
married Sarah Ann Parsons
(11/27/1873 to August 1952) in 1888
The children of Jason and Sarah Leslie:
Howard Leslie *(1889 to 1910)*
Frankie Leslie *(about 1891 to 1914)*
Jason Edgar Leslie
(9/3/1895 in Kansas to10/20/1967)
Roy Earl Leslie *(1898 to 12/1968)*

JOHN WILLIAM HAVENS
and **ANNA BELLE CARYLE**
John William Havens
(2/6/1854 to 04/xx/1903)
married
Anna Belle Carlyle
(1868 to 12/15/1889)
on xx/xx/xxxx in City, State
The children of John and Bell Havens:
Charles Henry Havens *(died at age 16)*
Lillie Mae Havens *(unknown)*

Following Theo Leslie's death, Sarah
Leslie's second marriage was to
Frank English
(about 1865 to xx/xx/xx)
in Joplin, MO.
The child of Frank and Sarah English:
Eva May English
(02/25/1909 to 1993)

Following Bell Havens' death, John
Havens' second marriage was to
Emma Alice Frakes
(1874 to 1954)
*(The family history of Emma Alice Frakes
is unknown. She was an orphan and
there is no record of her parentage.)*
The child of John and Emma Havens:
Bonnie Gladys Havens
(12/26/1896 to 2/2/1978)

Following John William Havens' death,
Emma Havens'second marriage
was to
John Carter
(xx/xx/xx to xx/xx/xx)
on xxx/xx/xxxx in Joplin, MO
The child of John and Emma Carter:
Christine Carter
(1906 to 1973)

JASON EDGAR LESLIE
and **BONNIE GLADYS HAVENS LESLIE**
Jason Edgar Leslie
married Bonnie Gladys Havens
on xx/xx/xx in Webb City, MO.
*The children of Jason and Bonnie
Leslie:*
Bonnie Katherine Leslie
(12/27/1916 to 8/11/1990)
Robert Edgar Leslie
(12/17/1920 to 5/5/1984)
Emma Margaret Leslie
(9/19/1921 to 12/17/1958)
Helen Maxine Leslie
(10/12/1923 to 11/22/1994)
John Theodore Leslie
(9/3/1930 to present)

FAMILY BIRTHDAYS

As a part of your research, you might want to make a report of family members like this example, sorted by birth month and date.

Name	Birth date
McKinley, Leslie Rena	January 9 1971
Byrd, Lisa Lucinda	January 16 1955
Leslie, Susan	January 19 1953
Leslie, Taylor	January 20 1995
Leslie, Paige Elizabeth	January 25 1993
Cochran, Kristian	February 2 1970
Byrd, Richard Wiley	February 25 1988
Leslie, Jeffrey Kent	March 13 1957
Weeks, Michael	March 20 1946
Leslie, Mark Jason Jr.	March 26 1983

Recording family names and birth dates is just the beginning. You can expand this list to include lots more information *(like physical address, marriage data, significant accomplishments, etc.)*.

If you do this work utilizing a spreadsheet program, you can sort it down in lots of different ways. After you've added address information to the file, Bingo!, there's your Christmas card mailing list. I'm sure you get the idea.

Of course, there are many software aids on the market today. Although they jazz things up a little, they all use the same data. But everything you do to record family information will be helpful in many ways. As mentioned before, here's a word of advice: don't duplicate information like this. Keep it all in one place. If you try to keep two files of the same information, one of the two will eventually be out of sync and you'll spend unnecessary time straightening things out

MAJOR FAMILY EVENTS

Someone needs to record significant family historical events because some day someone will want to know when "it" happened. An easy way to do it is to make a time line of major events in your family's life. By saving the date it happened, where it happened, and what "it" was, you'll be able to refresh your memory easily. I suspect an awfully lot of histories are written "by guess and by golly," because it's difficult to remember the year of occurrence, let alone the date. Some of the really important things that happened in your life are undated or, worse, unknown, to your family.

Remember that really crazy thing you did back in 1950? Or was it 1955? Only you know.

Keeping track of major family events starts with:

- Identifying the event
- The date it happened
- Where it happened
- And ends with a description of the event.

Examples of major family events:

50th anniversary	Heart attack
Your birth	Divorce
Baptism	Special honor received
First car	Won National Spelling Bee
Marriage	Second marriage
Birth of children	Military service
Birth of grandchildren	

A major family event is whatever you say it is. So make your selections and record them. However, do more than just write the event and the date.

Write the story of what happened. The story is most important.

PERSONAL TIME LINE

Your personal time line will enable you to relive your life. It becomes one of the important documents needed to prepare your biography and your obituary. It's logical that your record of major family events overlaps with your personal time line. Don't worry about it.

Here's an example:

1930 September 3	Birth of John Theodore Leslie at Joplin, Missouri
1930 October 9	Birth of Janice Marie Everhard at Rolla, Missouri
1950 September	John and Janice met at Joplin Junior College
1951 December	John & Janice engaged at Hidden Acres, Joplin, Missouri
1952 May	Janice graduated from Tulsa University
1952 June 6	Marriage of John and Janice

1953 January	John graduated from the University of Arkansas
1953 March	Moved to Trier/Bitburg, Germany with Air Force
1954 August 12	Birth of John Theodore Leslie II, Bitburg
1955 April	Tulsa, OK after discharge from Air Force
1956 September	Moved to Joplin, MO
1959 July 11	Birth of Mark Jason Leslie, Joplin, MO
1961 December 5	Birth of Douglas Robert Leslie, Bakersfield, CA

MEDICAL TIME LINE

This document is most valuable in your medical history, but checking it as you prepare your personal time line will make sure you haven't accidentally left out a significant event. Here's the example from Chapter 5, "Physicians and Prescriptions:"

DATE	EVENT
9/12/98	Heart attack. Got to the hospital in enough time that there was no damage to the heart muscle. Put a stent in my chest. Dr. Bruce Lachterman is my cardiologist now.
2/2001	Diagnosed with Prostate Cancer by Dr. Stuart Zykorie. Decided to self-refer myself to MDAnderson.
4/2001	Completed radiation treatments at MDAnderson under the supervision of Dr. Kuban.
5/29/2007	Had a TGA (Transient Global Amnesia). Had no short term memory for about 8 hours. Doctors could find nothing wrong, and I got my memory back.

EMPLOYMENT HISTORY

Does anyone know what a great employee you were? Or do they know the contributions you made to the profitability of a company? Do they know anything about the various jobs you had during your working career?

There is no example of an employment history in this chapter. Insert a copy of your most recent resume in your Going Away book and add any notes you want. If you spent your career with one company and never wrote a resume, just write a short work history, starting with when you joined the company and then describe the various jobs you had.

Years after your death someone is going to ask, "What did old what's-his-name do for a living?" A smart guy in the crowd will say, "Well, in his Going Away book he described his work. One of the things I remember the most is how he handled ...."

See?

VOLUNTEER AND SERVICE ACTIVITIES

You've probably made bigger contributions than you realize. Start back in high school or college. Did you belong to a group or club that had a service project? Maybe your group cleaned a stretch of highway or painted a house for an old widow?

Then, if you went to college, there were plenty of service opportunities, whether you were a fraternity or sorority member or an Independent. There were always plenty of things to do besides study. Don't exclude college service projects, because, as you remember, not only were they helpful, they were also a great way to meet pretty girls or handsome young men.

After you started to work, you may have joined the Jaycees Then later on, you joined the Rotary or Kiwanis Club or another of the many business and service clubs. Below is a "starter" list of volunteer services. There are probably lots of other organizations you can add.

Volunteer Organizations

Scouts	Adult Teacher/Discussion Leader
Church choir	Contributor to Church Policies
School Band	Wrote training manuals
School Orchestra	Chair, church celebration
School Choir	Outreach to patients in hospitals
School Debate	Team Lay Pastor
School Drama	Volunteer Counselor
Junior Chamber of Commerce	Member of Board of Directors, Civic Association
Suicide Prevention Counselor	Volunteer, Cancer support group
Member, Church Board	Big Brother Volunteer
Little League coach	Political Party worker
Volunteer Chaplain	
Member Young Republicans/Young Democrats	

Now, put together your own list and file it in your you know where.

PROFESSIONAL CONTRIBUTIONS

You'll have to decide what this section includes. Professional contributions are things like writing a textbook, making discoveries, being issued patents, being recognized for contributions to a city or an organization–different stuff from volunteer contributions. It's an important part of your life's story, but the details go all over the map.

You decide.

YOUR FAITH JOURNEY

Writing about your belief system and the impact your beliefs have had on your life is asking a lot of most of us. We go to church, visit with our friends, and then go home. It usually takes a personal crisis for us to examine *(or re-examine)* why we believe the way we do.

A lot of people don't even have a conscious belief system. If asked, what do you think most people would say? Probably, **"I believe in God,"** or **"My belief system is expressed in the views of the church I belong to."** If you're deeply religious (I am), finding the words to express how you feel about things and the moral code you follow is important. Putting it in writing is hard, but worth it. Your family and friends will appreciate what you've done. If you're not that kind of person, don't sweat it.

I would expect those who choose to express their faith and beliefs in writing would also want them to be a part of their funeral or memorial service. The service is a good place to share your faith journey and its reading will certainly impact on everyone.

PICTURES, MOVIES, DVD'S AND CD'S

There will be a time when your memories on film or disk will be very important. Most of us don't catalog our pictorial possessions, but we always talk about doing it someday. At the least, put the items that represent records of memories in a box that is clearly labeled. Be sure the pictures show the date, where the picture was taken, and who the people are. Consider having some of your pictures transferred to disk. That way, they don't fade and someone can watch them on their TV screen.

YOUR ON-LINE MEMORIES

Many persons (particularly younger ones) have an on-line presence through their participation in personal web sites and membership in blogs. Everyone recognizes "Facebook," but there are many other such places on the web where personal information can be stored. A growing number of people mourning loved ones can *(as reported in Time Magazine)* tap into a trove of memories by searching their loved one's online presence. Some computer sites have established a specific "memorial site" for profiles of deceased users.

If you're part of the growing numbers who make the digital move and record your life online, you're storing less away in dusty attics and leaving less hard copy for your loved ones to discover and hang onto. As Time says, "Letters have become emails; diaries have morphed into blogs; photo albums have turned virtual and come with tags."

If the pieces you put online are intended to be part of your legacy, investigate ways to collect it and save it permanently somewhere where it can easily be found. Who knows, in the future people may consider their digital assets properties to be disposed of in their wills. *(Check MySpace, MyDeathSpace, LiveJournal, Flickr, Deathswitch, and other sites that provide for screening and storage of internet data.)*

As you review your own computerized life, there are sure to be events you want to save, either for medical, personal, or family reasons. Once you've decided, make your file. Save it and update it periodically.

WHY DO ALL THIS?

Why prepare all this information? It's difficult to do, but here is why:

- It's helpful if you're ill; if you die, it's essential for your obituary. Your biographical data is the basis for your obituary
- No one knows you like you know yourself or knows some of the things that happened in your life.
- Writing your obituary is easiest done using data kept in orderly form and easily found.
- The information becomes a record of your achievements in life.

- It is a record of what you have enjoyed.
- You've lived an interesting life; people need to know some of the events that made you what you were.
- And, perhaps, it's a way to tell others of some of the pain you have experienced.

One last comment about this information you're putting together: It's OK to use your imagination as you record events. You are a storyteller and you want your story to be interesting.

Remember, it's all about you.

Cherished and Not so Cherished... Possessions

You need a plan for disposing of your possessions

At a church meeting a very wealthy man rose to tell the rest of those present about his Christian faith.

"I'm a millionaire," he said, "and I attribute it all to the rich blessings of God in my life. I remember the turning point in my faith. I had just earned my first dollar and I went to a church meeting that night. The speaker was a missionary who told about his work.

"I knew I only had a dollar bill and had to either give it all to God's work or nothing at all. Therefore, at that moment, I decided to give my whole dollar to God. I believe that God blessed that decision, and that is why I am a rich man today."

As he finished, there was an awed silence at his testimony. After he sat down, a little old lady sitting in the same pew, leaned over and said to him, "I dare you to do it again."

This chapter discusses the disposition of your possessions–those really valuable ones, the not-so-valuable ones, and those of little value. Deciding which is which is your job!

If you want to have a family squabble, don't make any decisions about the distribution of your assets before your death.

We're not talking about cash, stocks and bonds, or other assets with a relatively-easy-to-establish value. It's easy to divide up items with a market value that doesn't vary a lot day-to-day. It's your other possessions that will take up your time. If you don't set the rules for distribution of your possessions, family relationships will be stressed before the dust of your estate settles. I hope the wisdom of deciding what to do with your possessions before you die is apparent.

This process can start at any time; in fact, please do start right away. Stretch it out so you won't experience burn-out.

(A major project is coming up. You've talked about doing it for years. Maybe you're motivated enough now to really do it. We'll see.)

WHEN DO I START DISPOSING OF MY POSSESSIONS?

This is not an easy question. Everyone will have an idea of the best time to start, usually later. Here are the rules I suggest:
- If you're 75 years old or older, start this project now
- If you have received a medical diagnosis that indicates you may have problems ahead, regardless of your age, start now
- If you have idle time, start this project now
- If you don't fit the above categories, set a firm start date

HERE'S THE PLAN

When you've done everything in this chapter, you'll have your possessions categorized into four groups:
- Items not so valuable or of little value
- Garage/yard sale items
- Valuable and not-so-valuable things
- Really valuable things

ITEMS NOT SO VALUABLE OR OF LITTLE VALUE

In this chapter you will mostly be planning for events that will occur after your death. However, this first section covers something you can do while you're still alive.

Gather up all the things that are not so valuable or of little value to you. You don't have to make a list. Clean out your garage, your closets, your pots and pans, and your desk. It may help you do this if you convince yourself the things you don't want any more and no one in the family wants may prove to be a "treasure" to someone else.

Give the collection to a donation center (*like the Salvation Army, Goodwill, or a church-based organization*). You'll get a tax deduction. The charity will decide from the things you give them what has value to their organization. They'll keep them for gifting or resale and get rid of the rest. Can you do it?

GARAGE/YARD SALE ITEMS

This section covers the disposal of those things you usually see at a garage or yard sale. Of your possessions, you know what those items are. You've been meaning to have a garage sale for years.

Go through the house, room by room, and mark the items that you want disposed of in a Garage/Yard/Estate sale with a label of some sort. (*a sticky dot is good*). You should probably make a written list at the same time. (*Use the form at the end of the chapter, modified however you want.*)

The way these items will be marketed is not going to be discussed in this book. It's a subject every woman has talked about with her friends. All you have to do now is be sure someone will be responsible for having the sale or hiring a group that manages sales like this. There's not an easy way to say to someone, "Will you manage a garage sale of my stuff after I'm dead?" Go figure, I'm at a loss here.

Anyway, the garage sale things you've identified are now out of the way as far as planning goes. The only decision left is to decide how to distribute the cash from the sale. Easiest way is to simply divide it up—after the pizza and beer have been paid for.

VALUABLE AND NOT-SO-VALUABLE THINGS

This is a large group, too. You probably will not want to include these valuable and not-so-valuable things in your will. It will be easier to give them away. Moreover, if you wish, you can do this before you die! In this category are those things that have sentimental value, are antiques or period pieces that can't be bought just anywhere or are unique for any number of reasons. They're just not the stuff you'd bequeath in your will. You know what they are.

Disposing of these items will not be a problem if you follow the procedure outlined below.

The best way is to decide who gets what before it becomes a problem. If you haven't already done so, take an inventory. Inventory everything room by room. We're not talking about a whole lot of stuff; you've already eliminated the stuff you gave away and identified the things that will be sold in a garage/estate sale after your death. After this selection of valuable and not-so-valuable possessions, the only things remaining are the valuable items you will dispose of in your will.

You can easily take the inventory a little at a time if you confine your activities to one room at a time. Don't try to do your whole house in a day.

At the end of this chapter is a sample form to use to list the stuff. You'll notice there is a column for the story associated with the item. Write why you bought it, who gave it to you, who you inherited it from, or the unusual event that occurred when you got it. Of course, there's not an exciting event associated with every piece of furniture or picture or knick-knack. But, if there is a story you want everyone to remember, write it with the inventory.

Now the hard part. Who gets what from your inventory of items that are not included in your will? Here's one approach: at a family gathering, pass the list around and let everyone choose what they would like to have after your death. Reconciling choices is not easy with this method and I do not recommend it.

Here's another, better possibility: make a slip of paper with the name of an item on it (or the number on your inventory list); then pass the hat. Once everyone has taken the slips and knows what they've got, horse-trading begins. You don't have to be involved in that. When everyone has settled down, write on your list who gets the various pieces.

If everyone's lucky, everyone will still be friends after the trading is completed. The items will be distributed after your funeral.

Can you do it? If there are things left over, add them to the Garage Sale list.

REALLY VALUABLE THINGS

Who gets the really valuable things is still a project you can handle while you're alive. However, if you don't, someone else can easily do it, so don't worry. We're talking about furniture, china, carpets, silverware, pictures, lamps, jewelry, stocks and bonds, books, your house, cars, vacation home, etc., all things that are obviously worth something. But how much? Don't plan on putting a cash value on them; it'll drive you crazy.

Fair value. If it happens that you *(or your executor)* have to establish the value of a possession in order to insure fairness, don't do it yourself. Use a professional. Doing so allows you to be impartial. If someone questions the worth of an item, the response is "Such and Such Appraisers established these values based on their experience. We will abide with their estimates." That will stop bickering.

How do you keep everyone happy with the distribution of your valuable items you will specify in your will and bequeath to named individuals?

Here is a suggestion: Start out by listing on a form *(like the one shown at the end of this chapter)* all the valuable items you will mention in your will. Either decide yourself or ask those persons you want to have some of your possessions to identify three things from your list they'd like to have. Once that's done, repeat the process. Have them pick three other, not-chosen items. Repeat the process until you have a recipient's name on every item.

Go though everyone's list and decide what you'll do about those items chosen by more than one person. To break ties, draw high card; pick a number; play rock, paper, scissors; whatever. Your task is to eliminate duplications. Eventually, you'll finish this exercise and then you can specify in your will who will get what.

AN EASY INVENTORY LIST

Here's an easy way to list your items, tell their story and record who gets each. Draw the lines on an 8 1/2 x 11 inch pad.

IMPORTANT STUFF		

ROOM: Study
NOTE: Number the items to agree with the listing number

POSSESSION	THE STORY ASSOCIATED WITH IT	GOES TO
1 Ship Clock	This was a 1975 gift to me by the Occidental Petroleum staff at Geneva, Switzerland	(Name entered after item chosen)
2 Projector	I bought this for PowerPoint presentations.NS (stands for "no story")	

Good luck.

Anticipating YOUR final Days

You can't avoid it; here's a way to handle dying

A distraught senior citizen phoned her doctor's office. "Is it true," she wanted to know, "that the medication you prescribed has to be taken for the rest of my life?"

"Yes, I'm afraid so," the doctor told her.

There was a moment of silence before the senior lady replied, "I'm wondering, then, just how serious is my condition because this prescription is marked, 'NO REFILLS'."

This is an absolutely incredible short interview by Paul Bradshaw with Rick Warren, 'Purpose Driven Life ' author and pastor of Saddleback Church in California. *(Interview slightly edited and shortened. If your belief system includes God and Jesus Christ, read this; otherwise skip to the next section.)*

In the interview, Rick said:

People ask me, 'What is the purpose of life?' And I respond, "in a nutshell, life is preparation for eternity. We were not made to last forever, and God wants us to be with Him in Heaven."

One day my heart is going to stop, and that will be the end of my body - but not the end of me. I may live 60 to 100 years on earth, but I am going to spend trillions of years in eternity. This is the warm-up act, the dress rehearsal. God wants us to practice on earth what we will do forever in eternity.

We were made by God and for God, and until you figure that out, life isn't going to make sense. Life is a series of problems: either you are involved in a problem now, you're just coming out of one, or you're getting ready to go into another one. The reason for this is that God is more interested in your character than your comfort. God is more interested in making your life holy than He is in making your life happy. We can be reasonably happy here on earth, but that's not the goal of life. The goal is to grow in character, in Christ likeness.

I used to think that life was hills and valleys— you go through a dark time, then you go to the mountain top, back and forth. I don't believe that anymore. Rather than life being hills and valleys, I believe it's kind of like two rails on a railroad track, and at all times you have something good and something bad in your life. No matter how many good things are in your life, there is always something bad that needs to be worked on.

And no matter how bad things are in your life, there is always something good you can thank God for. You can focus on your purposes, or you can focus on your problems.

If you focus on your problems, you're going into self-centeredness, which is 'my problem, my issues, my pain.' But one of the easiest ways to get rid of pain is to get your focus off yourself and onto God and others.

You have to learn to deal with both the good and the bad of life.

Am I going to be driven by pressures? Guilt? Bitterness? Materialism? Or am I going to be driven by God's purposes (for my life)?

YOUR FINAL DAYS

How soon before your "final days" begin?

You don't know?

Most of us will be surprised to hear the words, "your illness is terminal." After the shock wears off, it's pretty normal to think, "I'm not ready."

Eventually, questions like these come up:

What will happen after I die?

How will my death come?

What should I do to prepare?

Will I outlive my money?

Will my spouse be able to get along?

Will my children take care of my spouse?

Will they fight over my estate?

Have I done enough good in my life? *(You can depend on God's forgiving grace.)*

Since you're reading this and you're still alive, it's not too late. Address your concerns and your fears.

DO SOMETHING! NOW!

What should I do first? Remember the thirds of life:

0 to 30 years

30 to 60 years

60 to 90 years

You're probably in the last third of life, somewhere between 60 and 90 years old. And you still have lots of things to do before you die.

Do you believe life goes through defined phases? Those who do believe life's phases go something like this:

One to 30	Birth
	Education
	Work
30 to 60	Work
60 to 90	Work
	Retirement
	Live at home or move somewhere else
	Retirement life style
	Illness

Hospital care, followed by
In-home living (alone or with care)
Nursing Home
Assisted living
Extended care facility
Hospice
Death

It's in the last third of life where all the bad stuff happens. Things begin to change in this period, sometimes too fast. Do you recognize the changes? You move a little slower, get tired easier, hurt when you get up from your chair, take prescription medicines everyday, and you probably have at least one complaint now you didn't have last year.

Let's face it: as good as you are today, you're not as good as you were 10 years ago. Right? Perhaps it's time to:

RECOGNIZE AND ACCEPT YOUR LIMITATIONS

Aging events will alter the way you live. Other than your age, how will you know you're entering the last third of life?

Have you noticed:
- With age, there are some changes occurring with your body's shape. You're "settling and spreading."
- The way you do some things today and the speed with which you do them differs from the way you "used" to do them.
- Life style adjustments may be necessary and, in fact, are happening.
- Age has altered the way you live.
- You now—or will soon—need assistance of some kind.

It's one thing to talk about final days in general terms. But how would you feel if you knew that at the end of "X" months you would have a major illness or that you would die?

It's true. Something will happen to you one of these days. You just don't know the years or months that "X" represents.

This is not morbid. Think about it: what event could happen to you that would create a requirement for you to depend on someone else to help you accomplish the daily tasks of life?

Can you accept the inevitable that dependence, in some form, will happen? If you can be a gracious receiver of help from others, it will be much easier on everyone. **"Easier on everyone"** means you, your caregiver, doctors, nurses, family...everybody.

Maybe you should consider giving your loved ones an intervention letter, called in this chapter a **"No Burden Letter"** *(first discussed in Chapter 8).* You should also consider writing a **"Letter of Permission."** The letters enable others who recognize changes are occurring, particularly mental changes, to tell you and suggest a plan of action. It's quite possible these changes are occurring and you're not aware of them. If you don't want to give them such a letter now, at least write the letter and save it for later.

Keep going. Examples of the letters from the other chapter follow *(just in case you don't remember!).*

NO BURDEN LETTERS

Here's the "No Burden" Intervention letter:

```
Dear Family,

As we have discussed from time-to-time, we have
witnessed in either our friends' or family members'
behavior situations that appear to create the need
for personal safeguards or professional help.

This may happen to me.

Accordingly, I hereby agree that if any three of you
sign a letter to me and confirm to me in person your
concerns, I will address the issues you identify and
seek assistance.

Of course, if I'm absolutely bonkers, I'll probably
ignore the whole thing. In that case, someone else
will have to take action when I'm unable to recognize
the need.

Lovingly,
```

PERMISSION LETTER

And here's the "Permission" letter:

```
To My Dear Family,

At the time I am approaching the end of my life,
when I can no longer care for myself or make rational
decisions, I know I will be dependent on you or
someone you choose.
```

I want you to know that I give you the freedom to do what you think best for me as well as for yourself and others that are involved.

I would like to be attended to in a loving way (as I have described in other directives relating to my care), but I do not want you to sacrifice your health, your finances, or your relationships.

Accordingly, as the end of my life approaches and if I no longer know what I'm saying or doing, I might make unreasonable demands of you. Right now—while I am in my right mind—I want to say I do not expect you to give up your life for me.

Do the best you can to make me comfortable and pain-free. Doing so may mean I will live in an assisted living facility or nursing home. That's OK with me. I want Hospice to care for me in my final days.

This series of letters would not be complete without showing you a family's response to their father's "No Burden" letter:"

Dear Dad,

As you will remember, you asked us to notify you if we observed any changes in you that worried us. We have recently noticed a few quirks—little changes in your behavior that concern us. We view as a problem with potentially serious implications your actions of late, specifically:

    1. You have begun telling the same story four or five times in a row.

    2. Your toilet habits seem to be slipping and you are not bathing regularly.

    3. Remembering names is difficult for you, even your own children's.

We would like to have a specialist examine you. We have checked with your primary care doctor and he concurs in our recommendation. He has also provided us with the names of several specialists he knows and in whom he has confidence.

On this date, the three of us sign this letter in love.

What do you think about the letters? You'll do what is best in your specific situation, but it's always good to evaluate options.

LONG TERM CARE INSURANCE

Consider Long Term Care insurance. It's costly if you buy it when you're older. But it will cover some very expensive times in your life, times that could possibly eat up your savings. About 25% of people over 65 will spend a year or more in a nursing home. Check it out. Your insurance advisor will help you determine the cost/benefit of long term care protection.

CARE IN YOUR FINAL DAYS

How long before your final days start? How long will your final days last? Believe me, when they come you won't be singing, "Happy Days Are Here Again."

No one can really answer those questions with assurance. But the questions are coming down the road ... and they're picking up speed.

What kinds of care do you want in your final days?

Knowing what you want and then asking for whatever provides comfort are ways of taking charge. (*Examples: you want to comfortable, free of pain, around people you love, share memories, be touched by loved ones, and feel a sense of peace in safe surroundings.*) This important topic of care in your final days was discussed in Chapter Four; "Advance Directives," and is particularly well-described in the "5 Wishes" document.

Let your caregiver know the persons you would like to talk to or be with in your last days. The worst kind of loneliness is to feel alone when you're dying; you want to be with people you love.

Are you afraid because you don't know what will happen to you after you die? The unknowns are scary. Dying is a bridge between this life and the next; you know that. Most people say they are not afraid of dying, but they fear the dying process, the pain, and the separation from loved ones.

If you could face your fears, what would help you the most to overcome them? The answer to that question is different for everyone of us. Once you come up with your answer(s), put your written answers in your Going Away book, tell somebody and give them a copy of your list to handle for you if they can.

CAREGIVERS

Who do you want to be in charge of making you comfortable and pain free? Members of your family? A dear friend? Hospice? Write down the question and the answer(s) and give the list to somebody you love and trust and file a copy in your Going Away book. The names you write are undoubtedly the names you've put in your advance directives.

Based on what you write and say, the persons you've identified will make choices and select caregivers and other service providers. Of the names you've chosen, note those you would be willing to give legal authority. Of course, advance directives formally do this, but, just in case something unexpected happens, write the names down anyway and date the list. If you haven't already had a conversation with the persons named in your directives, do it. This is important.

SPECIAL NEEDS

Do you have safeguards in place that will make sure you're not taken advantage of? It happens, you know. Your directives should cover these eventualities; if they don't, talk to your attorney.

AGING OPTIONS

For the remainder of this chapter you'll have to put on your accounting eye shades. You may find this section boring, especially if you're in good health and have lots of money. Even though you may find this information tedious to read, there are gems in the following paragraphs. Knowing the choices *(and the answers to questions)* may enable your heirs to bless your name. . . and their bank accounts.

HOME HEALTH CARE

This is one of the best-kept secrets. Free home health care is available wherever you live if you are enrolled in Medicare or Medicaid.

MEDICARE

Medicare patients are provided free-of-charge nursing, bath aides, physical therapy, occupational therapy, and speech therapy. Other than the requirement that care must be prescribed by a doctor, the only other requirement is that the patient be home bound. The "home bound" test is that the patient not drive and, if leaving home for any reason, doing so requires a taxing effort.

Home visits by home health care personnel typically last about an hour. Extended periods of care *(several hours per day)* must be paid for by the patient.

Patients are re-certified every 60 days, meaning their physician must agree they require continuing care. There is no limit as to the number of times a patient may be re-certified for in-home care. *(At least this was the rule at this writing.)*

All health-related services are coordinated and overseen by the patient's physician. If physician office visits are difficult for a patient, in-home physician visits can be arranged by the home health organization.

Home health care patients are also eligible to receive Medicare-paid medical equipment, such as a hospital bed, wheelchair, bedside commode, or oxygen.

Home health care is unique in that it allows a Medicare patient to "self refer." This means a person is not required to be hospitalized first before receiving care at home. Homebound patients who require assistance performing daily activities or nursing care or therapy can contact a home health agency directly. The agency will then coordinate with the patient's physician to begin services. You can choose the home health agency you prefer.

Medicaid is a Federal/State program available to those who qualify, primarily based on financial situation. If you qualify, Medicaid can provide some in-home assistance *(called "Provider Care")* that authorizes you to receive up to 40 hours per week of caregiving service. For persons not yet eligible for Medicare, Medicaid may also provide assistance with prescriptions and medical care costs.

It is possible to be on both Medicaid and Medicare and to receive services from both programs simultaneously. When any duplication of service occurs, Medicare will be deemed to be your primary provider.

Your state Aging and Disability office sets Medicaid eligibility guidelines. Some states require some repayment to the Medicaid program for services rendered if you die leaving an estate.

LIVING ON YOUR OWN

You will be most independent if you live out your life in your own home. Most aging services are available to you in your home. An alternative is to move to a smaller place that requires less "taking care of." Your health and personal finances will determine your "living on your own" choices.

RETIREMENT FACILITY

A retirement facility is a great place to retire to because you'll immediately have friends around your age with similar interests. Practically anything you might want is available. It's costly, so most retirement home residents have a source of income beyond Social Security.

The physical arrangement of a retirement facility can be as complex as multi-story apartments with all amenities provided, a "villa" in a retirement village, or a place you acquire on your own, either as a renter or owner. You've probably been bombarded with advertisements, so you can tell there are lots of choices. Medicare services are available to you in any of these living arrangements. You can also purchase "extra-charge" services not covered by your insurance.

ASSISTED LIVING

An assisted living facility provides more personal care than a retirement facility does, but not as much as a nursing home provides. Assisted living is characterized by independent living and limited medical and other care assistance. In this life style choice, residents are provided planned activities, housekeeping and laundry services, transportation by facility-owned vehicles, meals, exercise, wellness programs, opportunities to socialize with other residents, and assistance with the activities of daily living such as bathing, toilet use, eating, dressing, and may include services like medication reminders.

Assisted living enables seniors to age-in-place in a communal living environment. Assisted living avoids premature transfers to more intrusive and costly housing/service options (*like a nursing home*). An assisted living facility provides group care for a person who cannot remain in a private home setting. Generally, single rooms or small apartments are set up to encourage independent living. Residents are expected to do many things without assistance. Residents do not require the care provided in a traditional nursing home where 24-hour care is provided by licensed or registered nursing staff (*in a skilled nursing facility*) or by certified nursing assistants (*in an intermediate care facility*). Most assisted living facilities are licensed by a state agency as an adult care home.

A home health care agency of your choice can provide medicare services in this living arrangement.

Note: In addition to assisted living facilities, other housing options included in this type service include residential health care facilities, boarding care homes, adult family homes and intermediate personal care homes. In all likelihood, new types of services are being created every day.

NURSING HOME

Full medical care is typically provided in a nursing home. At this writing, Medicare pays for the first 20 days' residence, then patients are required to pay an additional daily rate to supplement Medicare's payments. After 100 days, the patient is required to pay all costs. This is where long term insurance kicks in and covers most expenses.

A **"nursing home"** *(also known as a "convalescent home," Skilled Nursing Unit ("SNU"), or "rest home")* is a place of residence for people who require constant nursing care and have significant deficiencies with the activities of daily living. Residents include the elderly and younger adults with physical or mental disabilities. Following an accident or illness, eligible adults 18 or older can stay in a skilled nursing facility while receiving physical, occupational, and other rehabilitative therapies.

The program does not cover nursing care if only custodial care is needed. *(for example, when a person only needs assistance with bathing, walking, or transferring from a bed to a chair.)* To be eligible for a Medicare-covered skilled nursing facility *(SNF)* care, a physician must certify that the patient needs daily skilled nursing care or other skilled rehabilitation services that are related to hospitalization, and that these services, as a practical matter, can be provided only on an inpatient basis.

A "Skilled Nursing Facility" (SNF) is either:

• A **"nursing home"** certified to participate in, and be reimbursed by Medicare. *(Medicare is the federal program primarily for the aged who contributed to Social Security and Medicare while they were employed.)*

• A **"nursing facility"** *("NF")* certified to participate in, and be reimbursed by Medicaid. *(Medicaid is the federal program implemented along with the state to provide health care and related services to those who are "poor.")*

Each state defines poverty and, therefore, Medicaid eligibility. Those eligible for Medicaid may be aged, disabled or children. In the United States, each state "licenses" its nursing homes, making them subject to the state's laws and regulations. Nursing homes may choose to participate in Medicare and/or Medicaid. If they pass an inspection, they are "certified" and subject to federal laws and regulations. All or part of a nursing home may participate in Medicare and/or Medicaid.

Nursing homes which participate in Medicare and/or Medicaid, are required to have licensed practical nurses *(LPNs) or "vocational nurses" or "LVNs")* on duty 24 hours a day. And, for at least 8 hours per day, 7 days per week, there must be a registered nurse on duty. Nursing homes are managed by a Licensed Nursing Home Administrator.

Skilled Nursing Facility (SNF) services may be offered in a free-standing or hospital-based facility. A free-standing facility is generally part of a nursing home that covers Medicare SNF services as well as long-term care services for people who pay out-of-pocket, pay through Medicaid, or through a long-term care insurance policy.

Medicaid also covers nursing home care for certain persons who require custodial care, meet a state's means-tested income and asset tests, and who also require the level-of-care offered in a nursing home. Nursing home residents typically have physical or cognitive impairments and require 24-hour care.

The cost of staying in a nursing home can be several thousand dollars per month. Some patients deplete their resources on the high cost of care. If eligible, Medicaid will cover continued stays in a nursing home for life. However, it is required that the patient be "spent down" to a low asset level first by either depleting their life savings or asset-protecting them.

HOSPICE

Hospice can serve as a caring shepherd on life's last journey and can add dignity and peace to life's closure. Hospice is a program of care and support for the terminally ill and their family. It represents the "gold standard" of care for those who are dying.

Hospice services are available when a person will no longer benefit from curative treatment. This means that the doctors know of no other treatment that might save a life. The general rule is that a person's doctor has referred the person to Hospice because their life expectancy is six months or less.

The goals of a hospice organization are to allow patients to:
- Remain in familiar surroundings, if possible
- Be in control of their lives as long as possible
- Be pain-free
- Die with dignity

Hospice personnel are trained in caring for those who are dying. In this regard they:
- Provide humane and compassionate care for people in the last stages of incurable disease or illness so they may live as fully and comfortably as possible
- Try to improve the quality of life–to make the best of each day during the last stages of life
- Embrace a philosophy of care that accepts death as the normal and final stage of life
- Enable patients to continue an alert pain-free life and to manage their other symptoms so their last days may be spent with dignity and quality, surrounded by loved ones
- Affirm life
- Do not hasten nor postpone death
- Treat the person rather than the illness
- Focus on quality of life rather than length of life
- Are family-centered
- Involve the patient and the family in making decisions

If a person in the hospice program gets better or their disease goes into remission, they can leave the program and go into active treatment. If their condition subsequently worsens, they can return to the hospice program.

The costs of hospice treatment are paid by Medicare, Medicaid, the VA, most private insurance plans, HMO's and other managed care organizations. Gifts to the hospice organization allow hospice personnel to provide free services to those who cannot afford it or to charge patients according to their ability to pay.

Hospices are regulated by the federal government and each state; as a result, standards are enforced, but services may vary from state to state. If you are looking for a hospice care giver, the best resource is a friend who has used one recently for a family member. Failing that, look for these qualities:

- Look at their brochure; what services do they provide?
- What is their procedure for pain control?
- Review the credentials of the hospice team. How were they trained and do they receive on-going training?
- What are the credentials and experiences of the person who will offer emotional and spiritual support?
- Are they clergy or mental health professionals? They should be
- How long has the agency been in business? Have there been complaints filed with the state?
- Do they have experience with the illness you are concerned about?
- Does insurance or Medicare/Medicaid cover their charges?
- Do they have a residential facility for patient care?

THINGS YOU WANT TO DO BEFORE YOU DIE

Remember the movie, "The Bucket List?" Jack Nicholson and Morgan Freeman, stars of the movie, play two terminally ill men with very dissimilar personalities. While in the hospital, they create a plan to live life to the fullest before they die. They made a list which they referred to as their "bucket list" of things to do before they "kick the bucket." Here's their list:

1. Witness something truly majestic
2. Help a complete stranger for a common good
3. Laugh till I cry
4. Drive a Shelby Mustang
5. Kiss the most beautiful girl in the world
6. Get a tattoo
7. Sky dive
8. See the Pyramids
9. Spend a week at the Louvre
10. See Rome

Do you have a list like that? You should.

Here's another person's list of things to do that they haven't yet done:

- Before July of this year make a list of people I want to thank for their friendship and for what they have meant to me and write each of them a personal letter.
- I want to mend broken fences. I want to say to the people I've hurt, "I was wrong. I hurt you. Please forgive me." Their names are on the attached list in my Going Away book. Either write them, call or personally visit each.
- I want to say, "I love you and appreciate you" to my family and friends in a special way. I don't yet know how I'll do this. Keep thinking about it until I get it figured out.
- I have written on a list the names, addresses and phone numbers of persons who have information about me they might want to share after my death. I'll ask them this year if they would eulogize me at my service.
- Share my financial affairs with my children this year.
- Update my will; share the contents with the children. Also, write a "loving letter" to be read before the will is opened. Start on it this year; update it annually.
- Make a list of the people I want to visit. Start doing it this year.
- Make a list of the people I want to visit me. Invite at least one or two of them this year.
- Begin organizing my files this month so I can put them in my "Going Away" book.
- Begin a list of memories, beliefs, dreams, and stories I'd like to pass on to my children and grandchildren.
- Prepare my list of possessions to give to others. Give them away this year.
- Get rid of things others wouldn't want and which I no longer need. Start this month.
- Plan a European river cruise for next year. Make reservations before Thanksgiving.

Now, start your own list. Update it as you identify other things you want to do before you die.

Here's the final piece of advice regarding your list: set a completion date for each item. Establishing a deadline will be an additional motivator.

Put your list in your Going Away book or on a page in your notebook *(If you can't think of things to put on your list, at least write "Special Things I Want to do before I Die" in your notebook. Date it. Refer back to the list occasionally; add things to your list and detete the things you've done or which you no longer have an interest.)*

Dying...

Understanding what's involved may help

If I knew it would be the last time
I'd see you fall asleep,
I'd tuck you in more tightly
and pray to God, your soul to keep.

If I knew it'd be the last time
I'd see you walk out the door,
I'd give you a big hug and kiss
and then call you back for more.

If I knew it would be the last time
I'd hear your voice lifted up in praise,
I'd videotape all the songs you sang,
and play them back day after day.

If I knew it would be the last time
I could take an extra minute;
I'd stop and say "I love you,"
instead of assuming you know I do.

If I knew it would be the last time
I'd be there to share your day…
But I knew we'd have so many more,
I could let just this one slip away.

For surely there's tomorrow
to make up for an oversight;
and don't we always get a second
chance to make everything just right?

Won't there always be another day
for me to say "I love you?"
And certainly another chance
to ask, "Is there anything I can do?"

But just in case I might be wrong,
and today is all I get,
I'd like to say how much I love you.
And I will never forget

tomorrow's not promised anyone,
young or old alike.
Today may be the last chance you'll get to
hold your loved ones tight.

So, don't wait until tomorrow.
Why not do it today?
For if tomorrow never comes,

you'll surely regret the day
you didn't take the extra time
for a smile, a hug, or kiss.
Or think you were too busy for what
turned out to be their one last wish?

So hold your loved ones close,
and whisper in their ear.
Tell them how much you love them and
that you'll always hold them dear.

Take the time to say, "I'm sorry," "Please
forgive me," "Thank you," "It's OK."
And if tomorrow never comes,
you'll have no regrets about today.

A friend of mine opened his wife's underwear drawer and picked up a silk-paper wrapped package. "This," he said, "isn't any ordinary package." He unwrapped the box and stared at the silk slip.

"She got this the first time we went to New York, 8 or 9 years ago," he said to himself. "She has never put it on, was saving it for a special occasion. Well, I guess this is it." He went to the bed and placed the gift box next to the other clothing he was taking to the funeral home. His wife had just died. He turned to me, a life-long friend, and said, "Never save something for a special occasion. Every day in your life is a special occasion".

As his female friend, those words changed my life.

Now I read more and clean less. I sit on the porch without worrying about anything. I spend more time with my family, and less at work.

I understand that life is a source of experiences to be lived up to, not survived through. I no longer save anything for use sometime in the future. I use crystal glasses every day... I wear new clothes to go to the supermarket if I feel like it.

I don't save my expensive perfume for special occasions; I use it whenever I want to. The words "Someday..." and "One Day..." are fading from my vocabulary. If it's worth seeing, listening to, or doing, I want to see, listen, or do it now. I don't know what my friend's wife would have done if she knew she wouldn't be there the next morning; this nobody can tell. I think she might have called her relatives and closest friends. She might have called old friends to make peace over past quarrels. I'd like to think she would go out for Chinese, her favorite food.

If I knew my time had come, it's the small things I would regret not doing. I would regret and feel sad because I didn't say enough times to my brother and sisters, son and daughters, and my friends, how much I love them.

Now I try not to delay or postpone anything that could bring laughter and joy into my life. Each morning I say to myself, "This is a special day. Each day, each hour, each minute, is special."

"YOU'RE DYING"

Hearing those words is a frightening experience. You feel sick, your knees buckle, you need to sit down before you faint, you can't catch your breath. Try as you can to understand, the words are unbelievable.

You knew you were sick–you haven't felt good for a couple of months. But you had no idea you were that sick!

The next obvious question to your doctor: "How much time do I have?"

Dying is discussed pretty frankly in this chapter

This handbook is not a primer on dying. The book's main purpose is to suggest things that you should consider before you get a grim diagnosis. Then, if you do get one, the things you've done in advance will make the end of your life easier for everyone.

Not easy, but easier.

There's always the possibility that you will die from an accident or from a medical event that kills you very quickly. In these kinds of death, it's those left behind who suffer. . . .

Face it, if you're in the last third of your life, over 60, you need to seriously consider completing the first draft of your Going Away book, and committing to updating it from time to time.

This chapter and the next discuss a person dying either at home or in a medical facility from an illness that lasts a while. In both chapters, the emphasis is on communications. In one instance, survivors are saying things to the dying person. And then, in the next chapter, you'll get a little insight into the mind of the dying person.

There's a natural sequence of events in this handbook. The chapters after Chapter 13 discuss the planning before and the events that have to be handled after death. In some instances, there are things that should be done before your death, but they fit into the general scheme of "after death" happenings. I hope all this makes sense. It will fall into place as you proceed through the chapters.

Dying is a process. I've tried to condense the writings of many authors down to a digest of the process and then proceed to suggest a few ways family and friends can be involved. The whole thing covers a very difficult period of time, but knowing what to expect may take away some of the fears and mystery.

Talking to a dying person is difficult. You don't have any idea of what's going on in their head, and they certainly aren't interested in your future plans. So what do you talk about?

Stay tuned.

WHAT HAPPENS AS YOU DIE?

This section is a summary; you may decide to skip it. If you stay with me and then subsequently decide you want to know more, there are lots of books and articles that describe dying. Google **"dying"** or **"death."**

There's enough in this chapter to give you an understanding of the process of dying. *(My objective is to help you learn the things that will make it easier on **your** survivors, nothing more, and I hope you do what is suggested far, far in advance of your last days. Dying, I might add, is not a cocktail party conversational topic.)*

The literature accepts these general time periods for defining events preceding death:

- One to three months before death
- One to two weeks before death
- Days or hours before death
- Minutes before death

Below are additional details regarding the events that occur within each time period. It starts with a summary of the process and then proceeds with a more-detailed commentary.

One to three months before death

- Withdrawal from the world and people
- Decreased food intake
- Increase in sleep
- Going inside of self
- Less communication

One to two weeks before death

Mental and emotional changes such as:

- Disorientation
- Agitation
- Talking with the unseen

- Confusion
- Picking at clothes

Physical changes such as:
- Decreased blood pressure
- Pulse increase or decrease
- Color changes, pale, bluish
- Increased perspiration
- Respiration irregularities
- Congestion
- Increased time spent sleeping
- Complaints of body being tired and heavy
- Not eating, taking little fluids
- Body temperature either hot/cold

Days or hours before death
- Intensification of the one-to-two-week signs
- Surge of energy
- Decrease in blood pressure
- Eyes glassy, tearing, half open
- Irregular breathing, stop/start
- Restlessness or no activity
- Purplish knees, feet, hands, blotchy skin
- Decreased urine output
- May wet or stool the bed

Minutes before death
- "Fish out of water" breathing
- Cannot be awakened

THE PHYSICAL AND EMOTIONAL ASPECTS OF DYING

Preparing for approaching death can be terrifying for the dying person, both physically and emotionally. Of course, the same is true for family and loved ones. There is in all of us a curiosity about dying. Regardless of religious beliefs, there have to be some doubts or shadows of uncertainty within each of us.

As the dying process enters its final stages, two different dynamics–physical and emotional–are involved as the dying person begins to fade away:

Physical Death

- The physical aspect concerns the body as it begins its final process of shutting down. This process was described above.

Emotional Death

- This emotional slipping away tends to follow its own priorities. Even when the body is trying to shut down (*the physical side of dying*), the spirit hangs on until a resolution of some kind is reached. To some, it may appear the dying person is "seeking" permission to go. Others believe the dying person needs to feel that those being left behind support and accept their approaching death. Once this "acceptance" is received, slipping into the next dimension of life can occur with grace and dignity.

Another author describes the dying process a different way. She calls them **"stages."**

THE STAGES OF DYING

- Denial
- Anger
- Bargaining
- Depression
- Acceptance

DENIAL

"I'm too young to die. I'm not ready to die." Of course, you don't just get up some morning and say, "Well, I'm ready to die today." Even when a physician informs you that nothing can be done, in the dying person's mind is the feeling that a mistake must have been made. The shock begins to ebb a little as you come to grips with approaching death.

How long will it take to acknowledge you really are dying, that death is just around the corner? It varies from person to person, of course, but there comes a time when one can no longer deny the inevitability of approaching death. Denying that it is happening won't work. The next emotion is understandable.

ANGER

You're angry! Realizing you are not in control of your life, or that your impending death has become a fact that sort of sneaked up on you has made you mad! You have no choice... you are going to die. You have always known one day you would, but no one had come out and stated it as a fact before. It makes you angry. You feel helpless.

Your anger is directed at everyone and no one in particular. You have lost control *(which is likely not a new feeling if you have endured a long illness)*, and you don't like it! Anger is normal *(if there is such a thing as "normal" in this phase of your life!)* and can become, in its own way, a strength. You can use your anger and the emotion and energy it creates to fight against the last part of your life. But it is a fight you will not win. After a while, the anger becomes debilitating.

Isn't there something else?

BARGAINING

"OK, God. Let's make a deal. How about compromising?" You promise God to do or not to do specific things if only you can be given more time. You use bargaining as the basis for living a little longer. For instance, you tell God:

- You want more time because of an upcoming event that is important to you
- You are suffering from insecurities regarding a member of your family or a loved one you feel is still dependent on you
- You need more time to heal a rift
- You need more time to say your goodbyes

Dying and "desperate" people become very creative as death comes closer. You won't go until these issues are resolved... You are eager to bargain with God.

If that doesn't work. . . .

DEPRESSION

You become depressed. Depression is a very normal part of the preparing-to-die process. You become depressed because of your inability to deal with responsibility, of uncompleted projects, acknowledgment that your attempts at striking a bargain have failed...and everyday life is not treating you very well.

You can't ignore the symptoms. The signs of terminal illness are there. Your mind and body are fully aware that your death is inevitable. You're aware, angry and filled with sorrow. And now guilt sneaks in as you mourn for yourself and the pain your dying is causing your family and loved ones.

Is there anything else you can do?

ACCEPTANCE

Acceptance comes reluctantly after you work though the numerous conflicts and feelings your upcoming death brings. There is nothing more you can do. You succumb to the inevitable as you become more tired and weak. You become less emotional. Calmness arrives and banishes fear. You realize the battle is almost over. And. . . it's really OK for you to die.

Acceptance of the reality that the physician's prediction was correct opens the door to the future and these other opportunities:

- You can now spend your time preparing for your death
- You can take care of that unfinished business; make it a priority
- Start telling loved ones goodbye
- Make amends

If you are in great pain and acknowledge death's inevitability, you may be under the care of Hospice. Hospice believes that death:

- Is not doing nothing; it is not defeat, resignation or submission
- Is coming to terms with reality. It is acceptance that the world will still go on without you, and that death, after all, is just a part of life

Another author describes the events of dying like this:

- Physical weakness / lack of energy / loss of interest in every-day things
- Withdrawal from family and friends / increased sleepiness / coma
- Loss of appetite

- Difficulty swallowing
- Confusion
- Restlessness
- Body temperature and color changes
- Breathing difficulties
- Lack of control of the body's bowel and urinary processes
- Unexpected alertness and increased energy
- Imminent death
- Clinical death

However the process works for you is what's important. And you, alone, make the rules.

Once the inevitable is accepted, what does a dying person talk about to those who will still be alive after his death?

See the next chapter to find out.

saying Good·bye

It's not easy

Live a good, honorable life. Then, when you get older and think back, you'll enjoy it a second time.

1. Two antennas met on a roof, fell in love and got married. The ceremony wasn't much, but the reception was excellent.

2. A jumper cable walks into a bar. The bartender says, "I'll serve you, but don't start anything."

3. Two peanuts walk into a bar, and one was a salted.

4. A man walks into a bar with a slab of asphalt under his arm, and says, "A beer please, and one for the road."

5. Two cannibals are eating a clown. One says to the other, "Does this taste funny to you?"

6. "'Doc, I can't stop singing 'The Green, Green Grass of Home.'" The doctor says, "That sounds like the Tom Jones Syndrome." Is it common? "Well, It's Not Unusual."

7. An invisible man marries an invisible woman. The kids were nothing to look at either.

8. Deja Moo: The feeling that you've heard this bull before.

9. Two Eskimos sitting in a kayak were chilly, so they lit a fire in the craft. Not surprisingly, it sank, proving once again that you can't have your kayak and heat it too.

10. A dwarf, who was a mystic, escaped from jail. The call went out that there was a small medium at large.

A mature, wise, and experienced lady wrote this:*

Old Age, I've decided, is a gift.

I am now, probably for the first time in my life, the person I have always wanted to be.

I sometimes despair over my body, the wrinkles, the baggy eyes, and the sagging butt. And often I am taken aback by that old person that lives in my mirror (who looks like my father!), but I don't agonize over those things for long.

I would never trade my amazing friends, my wonderful life, and my loving family, for less gray hair or a flatter belly. As I've aged, I've become more kind to myself, and less critical of myself. I've become my own friend.

I don't chide myself for eating that extra cookie, for not making my bed, or for buying that silly cement gecko that I didn't need, but looks so avant-garde on my patio. I am entitled to a treat, to be messy, to be extravagant.

I have seen too many dear friends leave this world too soon; some before they understood the great freedom that comes with aging.

Whose business is it if I choose to read or play on the computer until 4 AM and sleep until noon? Who cares?

I will dance with myself to those wonderful tunes of the 50's, 60's and 70's, and if I, at the same time, wish to weep over a lost love ... I will.

I will walk the beach in a swimsuit that is stretched over a bulging body, and will dive into the waves with abandon if I choose to, despite the pitying glances from the jet set. They, too, will get old.

I know I am sometimes forgetful. But, there again, some of life is just as well forgotten. And I eventually remember the important things.

Sure, over the years my heart has been broken. How can your heart not break when you lose a loved one, or when a child suffers, or even when some body's beloved pet gets hit by a car?

However, broken hearts are what give us strength, understanding, and compassion. A heart never broken is pristine and sterile and will never know the joy of being imperfect. I am so blessed to have lived long enough to have my hair turn gray, and to have my youthful laughs be forever etched into deep grooves on my face. So many have never laughed, and so many have died before their hair could turn silver.

As you get older, it is easier to be positive. You care less about what other people think. I don't question myself anymore. I've even earned the right to be wrong!

I like being old. It has set me free. I like the person I have become. I am not going to live forever, but while I am still here, I will not waste time lamenting what could have been, or worrying about what will be.

And I shall eat dessert every single day (if I feel like it).

(* I didn't write the little essay above and I don't know who did.)

It's safe to say everyone of us seniors has experienced the death of a loved one. If you were there when death occurred, you know it was an emotional event, filled with anxiety and remorse. The time before death is especially trying on everyone. This chapter covers some practical suggestions that will guide you through a visit with a dying person.

Sometimes minor medical problems become serious.

Sometimes no problems at all become serious medical problems. Even when everyone thought an illness was minor, sometimes something happens that causes death. This chapter begins with the assumption the person you are visiting knows they are seriously ill and may be dying. What remains uncertain is the time death will occur.

Does a dying person know they are dying? Maybe. Probably. Yes.

THE FINAL TRANSITION

While a dying person is conscious and aware, getting one's affairs in order includes working through deep emotions with friends and loved ones, including dealing with grief and bereavement. Unresolved family issues may become very urgent, with old memories and regrets pushing to the forefront. As the dying person gets closer to death, the time for dealing with unresolved issues is past. It's time to say goodbye, and there is little time to waste. Impending death destroys the illusion that there remains enough "time" to do things. There isn't. God will handle things from this point on.

Something happens to body and mind as the end comes closer. Before lapsing into unconsciousness in the period before death, a dying person experiences confusing emotions. Your task, along with all the others who are a part of the dying person's circle of friends and loved ones, is to make the final transition easy. As they leave their earthly body, they need to know they are loved, that their life meant something, that you will miss them, and that you'll see them again some day.

I hope you can do that for your dying friend or loved one.

VISITING A DYING PERSON

Visiting a friend or loved one who is in the last stage of life creates for the visitor insecurities and emotional problems like these:

- What do you say that will be comforting?
- What can you do to help?
- How do handle your own complex feelings?
- How do handle your own clouded perspective?
- Experiencing your own blurring prospect of death and life, does your grief cause communications to falter?
- Knowing that death creates problems for the dying *(as well as for survivors)*, what to do? What to say?
- How do you deal with the dying person's desire for closure, feelings of abandonment, isolation from the world around them, and the sense that their life has been a failure–all common emotional issues?

Too often we handle death by avoidance, by pretending there are no issues to be dealt with. We don't know what to say, so we say nothing. We don't know what to do, so we do nothing. Because of the guilt we feel, we avoid the circle of survivors.

This mindset is not good and you know it.

WHAT DO YOU SAY TO A DYING PERSON?

You've decided to visit your dying friend. You're visiting because you care. It's not easy to send a signal to your friend that you know he is dying, but if you can, and with both of you understanding the upcoming reality, then common ground has been established. Both of you will be better able to communicate.

Some very practical transition suggestions follow. When you come into the hospital room or their home:

- Don't say, "How're you doing?" Say, "You've been on my mind, I thought I'd come by and say 'Hello.'"
- Don't ask, "How're you feeling?" Say, "I'm concerned about you."
- Don't take gifts *(other than some necessities)*. Just go visit.
- Try to keep the visit as normal as possible.
- Don't talk about your personal health.
- Don't repeat gossip.
- As you enter into a discussion, remember, it's their life they're talking about. Listen.

- Avoid offering advice.
- Avoid judgment and criticism.
- Don't being up any subject that needs resolution.
- Avoid cliches and irrelevant conversation.
- If possible and practical, touch the person, even if they are unconscious.
- Notice things you can do: wash dishes, cut the grass, bring paper cups, towels, tissues, or a comfort pillow.
- Run errands.
- Encourage talking and reminiscing.
- Ask how they would like to be remembered.
- Give a warm hug, hold a hand, touch a shoulder; say something comforting.
- If possible, remind the person of their successes and what their life has meant to you. Avoid using the situation as a springboard to tell your own stories.
- Welcome tears–yours and theirs. Crying is normal and a healthy reaction.

You can't fix it. All you have to say is, "I'm sorry. I wish it were different." You don't have to know all the answers or solve all the problems.

Having a conversation may be difficult because the speech of the dying person is simply hard to understand. Do the best you can, but don't ask the dying person to repeat.

A dying person may be angry, resentful, scared, sad, resigned, accepting, or some combination of emotions. Don't judge what the person is feeling and saying, because that will probably stop the conversation in its tracks or make the person angry. Everyone dies differently. Some die fighting, others give up, and others die pretending they are not dying. There's no right or wrong way to die.

Many people find it hard to listen to people who are dying because in our society people always feel like they have to fix things. We all are familiar with the, "Don't just stand there, do something," mentality. Our natural instinct is to try to make the person feel better. In reality, nobody can fix this problem. But letting someone who is terminally ill express feelings without fear of judgment does help. If the person is angry, let him express it. Don't try to talk him out of his feelings.

It's best to just acknowledge feelings by saying:

- "It sounds like you feel angry," or
- "It sounds like you have some regrets," or
- "It sounds like you are scared."

After you have opened the conversational door, wait. When it is appropriate, make a greeting, and very carefully begin the conversation.

Don't bring up unresolved conflicts, estate problems, your needs or the needs of others. Some believe that giving permission to die is OK. Only say so if others in the room agree it's OK. If you are by yourself, use good judgement. Your friend or loved one is leaving, but it's a better place where they will go.

It takes a lot of courage to say, "I know you are dying and I don't want to upset you, but I'd like to talk about it. I'm wondering what your thoughts are now; I'd like to hear them." Invite the dying person to share their thoughts; **don't** share your philosophy. If you're scared about having the conversation, say so. Say, "I'm scared, but I'm willing to talk with you about dying." Be prepared to get a denial. He may not want to talk about dying; it may be too late. The dying person knows when the end is near.

But if you get a "yes," or a nod of approval, your role now is to listen, not talk. Asking meaningful questions is your contribution to this conversation. If the person is in denial or does not wish to talk about dying, respect that. He or she may not be able to cope with talking about death. Just let him know that the door is open. "I'll be here for you if you want to talk about it."

SHARING THE PAST

A dying person does some things that signal death is coming. For example, there is a tendency to reminisce. . .a lot. Remembering events of the past is a wonderful thing; in our later life we have much better recall of the good things that have happened; it's easy to forget our goofs and mistakes. Be prepared to hear again and again favorite stories. Don't worry if you're hearing the story for the umpteenth time, go ahead and enjoy it. Don't say, "Yes, I remember that story, you've told it to me before." Just listen and respond appropriately.

The dying person has a gift to give as they relate the stories of their youth and about the other people they have been connected with.

Reminiscing is a way to open their life to you. In all likelihood, the little anecdotes are very personal and you'll repeat them to others. It won't be too long before people will be saying, "Remember when she told us. . . ."

If you are a religious person, sharing your faith journey with one another may help. However, listening to their journey takes precedence.

ACKNOWLEDGE THAT DEPENDENCY WILL HAPPEN

A dying person cannot be self-supportive. As death approaches, the time has come to depend on someone else. If it comes up, your role is to be supportive–help your friend understand and accept that this is a time in life where others can really help. Depending on others is not a sign of insignificance. Remind the dying person that depending on others does not make a person worthless or inconsequential. Although illness has taken its toll, do what you can to prevent a dying person feeling hopeless. Others have been depending on him for years; he's cared for them, given of himself. Now it's his turn.

This is a time when your faith takes over. Depend on God. God's gifts come in many forms and the people who help other people are right up there at the top of the list.

You may be God's angel.

Your "Going Away" PARTY

Be prepared for when "it" happens.

Three friends die in a car crash, and they find themselves at the Gates of Heaven.

Before entering, they are each asked a question by St. Peter himself, "When you are in your casket and friends and family are mourning you, what would you like to hear them say about you?"

The first guy says, "I would like to hear them say that I was a great doctor and a great family man."

The second guy says, "I would like to hear that I was a wonderful husband and a school teacher who made a huge difference in our children."

The last guy replies, "I would like to hear them say, 'Hey look! He's moving!'"

We're back to the part of the book where you can take charge again. You're not dead yet!

At this stage in your handbook, you can acknowledge that you will someday die. Can you? Nod your head up and down if you agree.

Let's get busy. This chapter covers these topics:

- Developing the lists of people you want to be notified of your death *(you'll be entering data on your Instant Action form using supporting information and email lists, plus other lists of people that don't have email).*
- Making decisions about the events after your death *(like clothes to wear, disposing of jewelry on your body, how you want your body handled, and doing the preparatory planning for the celebration of your life).*

INSTANT ACTION REVISITED

Remember the form from Chapter 1, **"Instant Action on My Death?"** That document and some of the other forms already mentioned are going to be our guide for a while. And we'll do a little practical investigating. You'll be adding information like this to the Instant Action form you will create:

INSTANT ACTION TO BE TAKEN ON MY DEATH	
Family members to notify by phone. Other persons to be notified are listed in an email group called "On My Death," and on a list called "People to be Notified of My Death"	Funeral home or crematory and phone number to call to remove my body *(in case of an unusual circumstance like an accident, crime or suicide, the coroner or sheriff's office should first be called)*
Who will prepare and send the email	Burial instructions. Where more information can be found
Minister to call	Doctor to certify death
Two close friends to call for support	Personal attorney
Hospice *(if involved)*	CPA/Financial advisor
Contact the person who knows what I want done with my body	Life insurance agent

When you die, someone will look at your "Instant" form and start calling family members to tell them of your death and sending emails to others. So be sure to keep the list updated. When you become ill, in all likelihood someone will be in contact with this group and others who know and care about you and give them status reports.

TELL OTHERS OF YOUR DEATH

(I am assuming everyone has email these days. If some of your friends don't, follow the instructions for either the "persons to be called" or "written to" list.)

In your email software, create an internet distribution group called **"On My Death."** Don't wait until you're sick to do it. You probably already have most of the names that will be on this list in your Address Book. Insert the names and email addresses of these people, and add others to your distribution list. Review this list periodically and update it. Although this is a list of persons you want to be notified electronically when you die, there are other uses for it. For example, you may want to send them an occasional "update" on your health and other news of interest.

Print the list and put it in your Going Away book.

Be sure the name of the person at your church who handles death notifications to the congregation is prominently identified in your book. *(You might add that person to your email list, but a phone call notification should also be made.)* There are a lot of people who care about you and you want to be sure they know of your death.

If you have not yet done so, ask someone to be responsible for sending your notifications out and be sure their name is on your Instant Action form. They will send the email at your death and also send a letter to or call those persons who do not have email. If you would like your obituary included with both mailings, you need to prepare it. We'll be covering that topic later.

Below is an example of an email that could be sent to your list *(if your obituary has been prepared, it can be included as an attachment).*

Name of Houston, Texas died last night at 11:00 after a long battle with cancer. His body will be cremated.

A memorial service will be held at 11:00 Tuesday, month and date at Northwoods Presbyterian Church, 3320 FM 1960 West, Houston, TX 77068. After the service a light lunch will be served at the church. The family invites you to participate in this joyful celebration.

The Reverends Paul Nazarian and Ann Marie Swanson will officiate. Music will be provided by the church choir and a small brass ensemble.

You are also invited to join the family at home, 12345 Street, Houston, 77068, either before or after the service. If you want additional information, please call me at 281-555-XXXX

Here is an example of a few lines of a form you can use to list those persons who do not have email:

Send a Letter Notification of My Death to

NAME   *ADDRESS City, STATE, ZIP/PHONE*

_____   _____

_____   _____

HELPFUL ADDITIONAL INFORMATION

Now review the Helpful Additional Information form that you've filed behind your Instant Action form. Hopefully, you've already entered much of the data on the form. Someone else will supply the data that can only be provided after your death, but it all will become a part of your record for future reference.

Helpful Additional Information
(file with your Instant Action form)

1. Where my death occurred and the date and time of death
2. Give my jewelry for safe keeping to
3. Get 12 extra copies of my death certificate from the mortuary/crematory and file in my Going Away Book
4. Life Insurance Info located
5. Social Security death notification to
6. Veteran's info *(including policy if you have one)* located
7. Memorials from my estate to
8. Send notice of my death to these organizations
9. My draft of my Obituary info located
10. Place my death notice in newspapers and church bulletin
11. Pet care at
12. Provides child care
13. Has authority to pay bills
14. Places where out-of-town guests might stay
15. Utilities, Magazines, etc. address changes will be done by
16. Keys to house with

Discuss with your agents their responsibilities. Obtain their agreement to call or send an email to the persons you have specified and to send a letter to those persons who do not have email. Be sure the location of your lists is known by several persons.

If possible, have your obituary included with both the email and the letter mailings. Your friends will want to read about your life.

It may seem there's an awfully lot of forms and checklists. You're right, there are. I've tried to make things as easy as "1, 2, 3," and perhaps I've overdone the forms and lists.

However, I hope you're finding a difficult task easier and not requiring that you try to think through everything 'cause it's been done for you.

Below is a very personal checklist of things to start doing right about now.

THINGS TO DO NOW

- [ ] Make a list of those to be phoned right after my death and put it behind the "Instant Action" form which is filed in the front of my "Going Away" book
- [ ] Who I've asked to phone these people
- [ ] Create the email group address, "At My Death," and begin inserting names into the group
- [ ] Print a copy of the email list and file it in my Going Away book
- [ ] Who I've asked to send the emails at my death
- [ ] Include my obituary with the email if possible
- [ ] Send my obituary later by email, if necessary
- [ ] Start a list of those persons to be notified who **do not** have email, along with their mailing address or phone number, and file it in my Going Away book. Call it a "Letter Notification to Others of My Death"
- [ ] Tell everybody to include my obituary with the notification of my death, if possible

You want your death to be a celebration of a life lived. It's got to be a party!

Some of your friends may have died badly because they didn't see death coming, and didn't plan accordingly. A person can't know how long he will live, but preparing for your final exit will give you the chance to take charge and make important decisions. By thinking it through, your survivors will know your wishes when that time comes.

The checklist that follows *(another one!)* will enable you to express your preferences. Choose the statements you like and draw a line through those you don't. When you're satisfied, copy the statements you've chosen and put them in your Going Away book.

WHAT YOU WANT DONE AFTER YOU DIE

Choose what you want; ignore instructions that do not apply

i want my body

- ☐ Handled according to my Funeral Plan instructions
- ☐ Buried immediately
- ☐ Given to science
- ☐ Handled by this mortuary
- ☐ Prepared for viewing
- ☐ Buried following a service
- ☐ Buried in a casket described in my Going Away book
- ☐ Buried in an outer container described in my Going Away book
- ☐ Buried in this cemetery
- ☐ Cremated immediately without embalming
- ☐ Cremated, but embalming first is OK if needed

I want my ashes ☐ Scattered ☐ Kept in an urn at

My burial clothing

- ☐ If I chose a viewing, I want to wear these clothes:
- ☐ I want my body to be made up
- ☐ I want my glasses on my face
- ☐ I want to wear this jewelry
- ☐ I want to wear my fraternal and/or military insignia
- ☐ Before burial, remove my jewelry and insignia and give it to
- ☐ If I chose to be cremated, I want to wear these clothes

Viewing

- ☐ I want a viewing and visitation
- ☐ I do not want a viewing and visitation
- ☐ I want an "open" casket at the viewing
- ☐ I do not want an "open" casket at the viewing
- ☐ I would like pictures of special events in my life displayed at the viewing. The pictures are located

The burial service

- ☐ I want people to know my religious preference to be
- ☐ I would like the presiding minister to be
- ☐ I would like these ministers to assist in the service
- ☐ I want the scriptures I have specified read at my service *(regardless of the type service)*
- ☐ I want the emphasis in the service to be on my faith and my devotion to my family and friends
- ☐ I want the emphasis in the service to be on living a good life
- ☐ I want a formal funeral service in the church
- ☐ I want a formal service in a funeral home
- ☐ I also want a grave side service where those who wish may attend
- ☐ I also want a grave side service for family only
- ☐ I ONLY want a grave side service
- ☐ I want a funeral procession to the grave site
- ☐ I want an informal service, celebrating my life
- ☐ I want an unusual service, details of which are described in my Going Away book
- ☐ I want a memorial service at the church
- ☐ I want a memorial service at the funeral home
- ☐ I do not want the casket to be present during the service
- ☐ I want the open casket displayed during the service
- ☐ I want a closed casket displayed during the service

Music at my service

I want this type of music

☐ traditional religious ☐ contemporary religious

☐ classical ☐ country ☐ modern/jazz

I want the music performed by:

☐ soloist ☐ duet ☐ choir ☐ congregational singing

☐ jazz band ☐ string ensemble ☐ organ

☐ bagpipes

I want specific music played/sung *(the titles and other information are filed in my Going Away book.)*

Pallbearers

☐ The names, addresses and phone numbers of those I would like to be pallbearers are filed in my Going Away book

☐ The names of those I would like to be HONORARY pallbearers are filed in my Going Away book

Eulogies

☐ I would like eulogies by friends and other persons who wish to speak

Flowers or donations

☐ I would appreciate flowers.

☐ My favorites flowers are

☐ I would rather have donations made to

My obituary

☐ My prepared obituary is included in my Going Away book. I want my obituary printed in the following

☐ Funeral bulletin

☐ Church newsletter

☐ Hometown newspapers

☐ Social Organization newsletters

☐ High school alumni notice

☐ College alumni notice

☐ Fraternal publication

☐ Business publications

☐ Other

☐ Emailed to the list in my computer address book titled, "On My Death"

Guest book, gifts register, etc.

I want the Guest Signing book and the Record of Gifts and Flowers to be kept by

Special readings or visuals

I want a special reading *(which is filed in my Going Away book)*

☐ read ☐ included in the program bulletin

☐ I want slides or videos shown

Statement of my beliefs

☐ I want my statement of beliefs read *(the document is filed in my Going Away book)* and printed in the program

Reception following the service

☐ I do not want a reception after the service

☐ I want a reception after the service

☐ I would like the reception held at

☐ I want something else entirely which is described in my Going Away book

At the reception, I would like these events to take place

☐ Music ☐ Entertainment ☐ Other ☐ Food

Whew!

You'll change your mind and change things. Everything you do is dynamic. You're living in a "real time" world and nothing stays stable for too long. That's why it was suggested earlier to use a pencil and have a big eraser when you're making your lists.

Your Obituary...

Your last chance to let people know what a great person you were

Preparing your obituary is a "hard work" topic. If you choose to, you'll be using your work from the previous chapters and then ending in a blaze of glory with some creative writing... writing that will become your obituary.

GOOD ADVICE

The journey of a thousand miles begins with a broken fan belt or a leaky tire.

Don't be irreplaceable. If you can't be replaced, you can't be promoted.

Always remember, you're unique. Just like everyone else.

If you think nobody cares if you're alive, try missing a couple of car payments.

Before you criticize someone, you should walk a mile in their shoes. That way, when you criticize them, you're a mile away and you have their shoes.

Give a man a fish and he will eat for a day. Teach him how to fish, and he will sit in a boat and drink beer all day.

If you lend someone $20 and never see that person again, it was probably worth it.

A closed mouth gathers no foot.

Duct tape is like 'The Force.' It has a light side and a dark side, and it holds the universe together.

There are two theories to arguing with women. Neither one works.

Experience is something you don't get until just after you need it.

Never, under any circumstances, take a sleeping pill and a laxative on the same night.

YOUR OBITUARY: ONE OF A KIND!

If you were to pattern your obituary on what you see in newspapers, all you'd have to do is list your birth date, your death date and, maybe, the reason for your death. Then you'd start listing everyone in the family that survives you. Then you'd end, fireworks fizzling, with the listing of your dead relatives. Sometimes there would be a statement about work, military, or charities.

There's more to your life than just a recital of facts.

All the work you've done so far has been leading up to the writing of your obituary. Your friends are interested in the things you've done with your life, so write it all down. You can do a lot with the information you've gathered because, as you will discover, your obituary can be anything you want. A story makes easier reading.

A lot of preliminary-obituary stuff preceded this chapter. Here are the tasks you worked on in Chapter 9, "It's All About You," that should have gotten your creative juices flowing, and enable you to prepare a first-rate obituary:

- Your family tree *(the genealogy of your family)*
- Your family's birth dates
- Major events in your life
- Your personal time line
- Your medical time line
- Your employment record
- Your military career
- Your volunteer/service contributions
- Your professional contributions
- Your faith journey *(your belief system)*
- Pictures, DVD's, CD's movies

WHY WRITE YOUR OWN OBITUARY?

You will save your loved ones a lot of stress if you write your own obituary, at least up to the last year or so. A compelling reason is that you can say whatever you want without fear of contradiction!

There are other reasons:

- It's your personal record of your importance
- It enables you to be as creative as you wish

- It can include humor and special-interest stories only you know
- It reveals your true self

Now, while you're alive, start writing your own obituary. Here's how.

THE "TYPICAL" OBITUARY PROCESS

The "typical" obituary process starts with a statement about your death *(month, day, year),* followed by a cause of death *(if you want).* The newspaper style of obituary contains information like this:

Recent picture

Full name of deceased

Date of death

Cause of death

City, State, at time of death

Date of birth

Place of birth

Marital status

Spouse

Wedding date

Names of children and spouses

Names of grandchildren

Father's name

Mother's name

Brothers and/or Sisters

Funeral/Memorial service

If viewing, place it will be

Cremation or Internment at

Memorials and gifts

Education

Church membership

Church offices held

Committees, Task Forces,

Employment of significance

Honors / special recognitions

Public service

Volunteer organizations

Fraternal organizations

Special achievements

Military service

And on and on....

Running your obituary in a newspaper is very expensive. If you'd rather give that money to your heirs or a charity, only include in the paper the notice of your death and the funeral / memorial specifics. Run your full obituary in the funeral or memorial service bulletin and, additionally, email and mail it to your lists.

WRITING YOUR OWN OBITUARY

Your obituary should be the most colorful story of your life you can write, warts and all. If you've done the considerable preliminary work suggested in the earlier chapter, you'll have lots of resources to draw on. Remember, you're not writing a newspaper piece that simply covers the *who, what, where, when and how* of your life, but a recounting of the experiences of an exciting person – a person who has done things you want other people to remember! Your life is of interest, so write a story that people will find delight in reading as they sit in their pews, waiting for the service to begin. This is the article that will be pasted into scrapbooks and read again years later. This is the article that will be sent via email or letter to lots of people.

As you write, use the data you've compiled for your family tree, your current family birth data, major events in your life, your medical history, your work history, your biography—all the records you've created **and**...your imagination. Get additional information, recount serious or humorous events from your life, tell jokes, or share your wisdom. Make it as interesting as you can. Just because you've died, there's no reason for your "style" to change. If you enjoyed telling stories, tell some more. The people who read your obituary will say to themselves, "She was a story teller to the very end!"

You can do it.

OBITUARY EXAMPLES

What follows are a couple of examples of how it all comes together. In the first obituary, my friend agreed to let me share her very personal recounting of her life she wrote herself. Since she's still alive, I've removed all last names in case you know her and think she is dead. She isn't. She's still alive and kicking.

The second obituary is that of a dear friend who has died. His widow agreed to let me publish his obituary just as it was in the memorial service bulletin.

Both are presented just as written *(except for last names)*.

Betty Anne's Obituary

Betty Anne, a disciple of Jesus Christ, had eighty-five years of life experience before making her final earthly transformation on date, 2024. She was blessed with devout Christian parents, Elizabeth-Catherine and Rowland Thomas, who educated her in Christian schools in Philadelphia.

Betty Anne was the oldest of four children. She had three incredibly talented siblings, Joan Marie, Joseph, and Rowland, of whom she was very proud. Her family wintered in the Philadelphia main line town of Rosemont, Pennsylvania, and summered in Ocean City, New Jersey.

In September of 1957, following her graduation from the Academy of Notre Dame de Namur in Villanova, Pennsylvania, Betty Anne married Second Lieutenant Robert Lloyd. After a stay at Fort Knox, Kentucky, they relocated to Florida where she completed her freshman year at Palm Beach Junior College. Over the next years, Betty Anne provided support to her husband who acquired four advance degrees.

She spent three life-changing years at Princeton Theological Seminary. Betty Anne was married to the Reverend Doctor Robert Lloyd for twenty-eight years. They team taught the ninth grade communicant's class for years and led many youth group retreats.

For fifteen years, Betty Anne was a full-time mother to Lisa Anne (1960), Brent Rowland (1964), and Jamie Alexandra (1966) who were her precious gifts from God. Of her accomplishments, she was proudest of her three children. They matured into responsible and talented adults who are raising fine families of their own with the love and support of their spouses.

While her children were growing, Betty Anne was a Girl Scout Leader, Den Mother, Brownie Leader, 4-H Leader and involved in their church and school activities.

In 1975, Betty Anne fulfilled a promise to her parents by completing her Bachelor of Science degree and began her professional career in education and research. In 1978 she earned a Master's degree and in 1989 her doctorate from

Rutgers University. She was a member of Omicron Nu, Kappa Delta Pi, and Phi Delta Kappa honor societies. Betty Anne was very grateful for her years at Rutgers University.

Betty Anne's educational career spanned forty-three years and included several model programs. She was a high school teacher, high school vice-principal, and New Jersey State Supervisor of Education. She spent many years at Rutgers University where she directed statewide teacher-in-service, ModelNetics Management Training for school administrators, and the Northeast Regional Curriculum Coordination Network.

In her fifties, she studied in the field of gerontology and subsequently directed the Gerontology Program at Union County College in Cranford, New Jersey where she taught the Sociology of Aging and the Psychology of Aging. She later directed the Suffolk County Respite Care Program for Alzheimer's caregivers in New York. During that directorship, she was an adjunct member of the gerontology faculty at Long Island University where she taught Health and Aging in the graduate program. After relocating to Wellesley, Massachusetts, she was invited to be a visiting professor at Wheaton College where she taught Aging in America.

In 1993, Betty Anne became involved in the seminal work of the Spiritual Eldering Institute in Boulder, Colorado. She served on the Board of Directors, wrote the original Sageing curriculum, and was in the first group to be certified as Sageing Seminar Leaders. She conducted numerous Spiritual Eldering seminars around the United States.

In 1995, Betty Anne married Ivan Ramon in Wellesley, Massachusetts. They moved to Houston, Texas in 1997 where they joined Northwoods Presbyterian Church. Ivan was the love of Betty Anne's later life and they were fortunate to celebrate 15+ years of marriage. Betty Anne loved roses and Ivan brought her roses every month on the anniversary of their marriage. Their blended family of five chldren included Ivan's daughters Marianne, her husband, Carl, and Judie and her husband, Craig.

Betty Anne was Grammy to her ten grandchildren and she dearly loved them. She was blessed with six granddaughters: Sabrina Isham, Julie Alexandra, Emilie Elizabeth, Sophia Elizabeth, McKaela Quinn, and Abbey Logan. Her four grandsons are Bryan, Andrews Lloyd, Brent Andrew, and Kai Curtis.

Betty Anne spent many years in service to her Lord in the Presbyterian Church at the Presbytery, regional and local levels in three Presbyteries. She was the President of the United Presbyterian Women in two congregations. She was an active member of Northwoods Presbyterian Church and really loved the Celebration service.She served on a number of ministry teams at the Presbytery and local levels. She read her scriptures every day and loved working for the Lord. Betty Anne was a certified Bethel Bible teacher who taught the entire bible from Genesis to Revelation.

For two years she directed the model Sanctuary program for the Family Violence Center at Northwest Assistance Ministries and was devoted to her prison ministry. Betty Anne was the founding president of the Academy for Lifelong Learning at North Harris College. The Academy was an outcome of the Aging Texas Well research that she coordinated for the college.

Betty Anne was an avid reader. She enjoyed writing, playing in tennis leagues, making music on her organ, walking her Bichon dog, Sweetums, teaching short courses at North Harris College and facilitating Spiritual Eldering seminars. She was a member of the Friday Afternoon Ladies Literary Society (FALLS) for eight years, during which time she completed her book, Spiritual Elders: Women of Worth In The Third Millennium, her autobiography, and Ivan's biography. She looked forward to those Friday afternoons spent with her treasured friends with whom she shared much merriment.

Betty Anne's penultimate goal was to become a spiritual sage and she was working on that goal when she was transformed. One of her friends noted that for all of Betty Anne's life, she went like a woman with her hair on fire. Well, this week she finally went up in smoke! She died at x p.m.

The second example is a good illustration of the use of humor. The friends who gave eulogies at this fine man's memorial service all mentioned his love of a good story.

Ray's Obituary

Arthur Ray was born February 29th, 1944 in Corpus Christi, Texas, and died October xx, 2009. He was very proud of the fact he was so much younger than his friends (he had only one birthday every four years).

His family moved to San Antonio when he was three months old. At age eleven his family moved to Houston. He attended Pershing Junior High and Bellaire High School. In his home room he met Jeanie. In March of his senior year he asked Jeanie out for a date (please note she was the third girl he called that night). As it turned out, the third time was a charm, and they dated for the next three years. They were married July 10, 1965.

In November 1965, Ray quit his job. At the time he was working at the same place as his father and his father quit his job first.

His best friend told him Methodist Hospital was hiring in the Inhalation Therapy Department. He put his application in for a job at the hospital and also at the Houston Police Department. The hospital was hiring for work now and the police were hiring for positions starting the coming January. Ray went to work for the hospital in the Inhalation Therapy Department in December.

He loved the work and excelled. He had found his calling.

On October 4, 1965, Robert Arthur was born and Ray became a proud father. On March 11, 1970, Kathleen Denise was born and he was again a proud father. With Kathleen's red hair and winning personality she was able to wrap her father right around her little finger.

When Dr. Debakey did his first heart transplant, Ray was one of only two therapists that were cultured germ free and allowed to take care of the patients, a significant honor.

In the early 70's, the name of the department was changed to Respiratory Therapy. The nurse who had been running the department retired and Ray was named the Director. He held that position until the mid 80's. He was burned out and needed a change. However, Methodist Hospital didn't want to lose him, so they offered to let him keep the parts of the job he enjoyed, which was doing in-services, evaluating new equipment, ordering supplies and handling special projects.

He enjoyed not doing budgets. He loved his new job, often remarking "he would never retire." Unfortunately, Ray's health problems caused him to retire December 1, 2007. He had worked for Methodist 42 years.

He loved music of all kinds and was a World War II history buff. His family often accused him of being able to open either a music store or a bookstore because of his large collections.

We will miss him and his humor very much.

Burial OR Cremation?

Information to help you make the choice

Dying, a tough old cowboy counseled his grandson that if he wanted to live a long life, the secret was to sprinkle a little gunpowder on his oatmeal every morning.

The grandson did this religiously and lived to 93.

When he died, he left 14 children, 28 grandchildren, 35 great grandchildren and a 15-foot hole in the wall of the crematorium.

There are two issues involved in making the decision to be buried or cremated. One of the issues is easy: do you have deep feelings about one or the other? The other issue is whether the difference in costs is important?

Burial costs typically include the use of a funeral home's services. Their charges *(which are substantial)* start at the time they pick up the body for delivery to their facility.

Cremation costs include picking up the body, cremating it, and returning the ashes in a container *(which can be a cardboard box)*.

There are many options after you've made the decision to be buried or cremated:

- Use a "regular" funeral home
- Use a funeral consultant or advisor
- Veteran's burial
- Prepaid burial societies or groups
- Discount suppliers and "green services"

This chapter covers the two burial alternatives, burial and cremation, and then discusses various options, most of which apply to either the burial or cremation choice.

FUNERAL HOME SERVICES

Funeral Home managers are skilled professionals who do excellent work. They also have developed many cost areas, which the law requires they, when asked, itemize for families who use their services.

Keep a cool head when reviewing services offered. Check everything. If there are services your family or friends could perform, don't ask the service provider to do them. Following is a typical listing of the various for-fee services performed for clients *(and there are probably others)*:

Administration fee
Fee for basic services
Death certificate(s)
Transportation

- To Funeral home
- To another facility
- Flowers to cemetery
- Casket to cemetery
- Family to cemetery
- Flowers to church
- Police escort
- Family car(s)

Body preparation

- Embalming
- Bathing
- Cosmetology
- Casketing
- Refrigeration
- Hair
- Dressing

Funeral service facilities

- Visitation per day per room
- Minister
- Memorial book/cards
- Grave site service fee
- Cemetery plot
- Casket
- Vault liner
- Marker
- Installation of monument
- Chapel
- Guest registration
- Church service fee
- Burial expenses
- Opening/closing grave
- Vault
- Mausoleum
- Inscription per letter
- Video

Cremation costs

- Cremation urn
- Earth burial
- Columbarium burial
- Marker
- Inscription per letter
- Scattering
- Mausoleum
- Installation of marker

Flowers

- Purchase
- Memorial package
- Floral art

Obituary Printing

- Preparation
- Inclusion of picture
- Placement

FUNERAL CONSULTANTS AND ADVISORS

When dealing with a funeral home, the average consumer does not know all their options or what questions to ask.

Consultants, known as "service advisors," provide information to consumers and negotiate with funeral homes on their behalf for a fee. Funeral directors are required by law to provide price information to anyone who inquires by telephone or in person. While funeral directors are under no obligation to reduce prices, when asked, they may do so as a courtesy to families. Advisors know of other ways to reduce costs, such as using a veteran's cemetery rather than purchasing a more expensive plot in a cemetery. Ofttimes, survivors are afraid that if they do not spend a lot of money, their family will judge them negatively for selecting lower cost arrangements.

As a way to justify their services, service advisors tell clients funeral establishments have extremely different price ranges, and, because competition is heavy, the advisors take advantage of the competitive situation and negotiate with each funeral home. *(There is general agreement that many funeral homes have a "no walk" policy, which is a commitment to not losing any service opportunities. As a result of their negotiations, advisors familiar with the market refer families to cheaper funeral homes who provide a quality service.)*

The "advisor" process begins when a family member contacts a service advisor to discuss their expectations. The advisor then finds a funeral home and cemetery he feels will suit the family's needs and negotiates the price before the family ever visits the funeral home or speaks to funeral home staff.

In order to insure a quality service, the advisor first talks with the funeral home management personnel, then with other local businesses in the town to learn what other people think about the various funeral establishments. He also evaluates other factors, such as the size of the funeral home chapel, the age of the funeral cars, or whether the business is part of a large corporation or family run.

Not all advisor firms charge a fee for their services. Some charge on an "honor system," relying on a "personal honesty pledge" where consumers agree to pay a percentage of the amount saved.

Another approach, called "funeral concierge service," provides services by trained, knowledgeable advisors dedicated to ensure clients and their families receive personalized assistance to prepare for and deal with all aspects of a funeral. Concierge advisors do not sell or provide funeral goods or services; consequently, they are not required to be licensed. These advisors discuss with clients pricing options in much the same way as do other advisors, ministers, hospice workers, and attorneys. Typically, the advisors do not make funeral arrangements, but rather help outline clients' wishes so that they can be communicated in writing to the funeral home that is eventually selected. Their service charge is a onetime fee that does not vary with the complexities or expense of a particular funeral.

The concierge process follows these general steps:

1. The family contacts the funeral concierge service.
2. If the consumer makes their "wishes" clear, the advisor reviews the funeral plan with the family members.

3. Knowing what the consumer wants, the advisor gathers price comparisons from funeral homes and reviews the options with the family.

4. Once final funeral service decisions are made, the advisor communicates with the funeral home and acts as an advocate for the family.

5. Advisors assist with the cemetery and monument choices and provide aftercare by referring clients to sources of bereavement support.

There are funeral information sources available to consumers, such as the Funeral Consumers Alliance (FCA), AARP, and the Federal Trade Commission (FTC).

VETERANS' BURIAL SERVICES

The U.S. Government provides veterans a burial spot in one of the 130 national cemeteries *(for burial or inurnment)* and a ceremonial burial service. This is a considerable saving over normal burial expenses. Many of these services are available if a veteran chooses to be buried in a private cemetery. *(Benefits are restricted to a government headstone or marker, a burial flag, and a Presidential Memorial Certificate. Benefits are not available to spouses and dependents buried in a private cemetery.)*

Requests for burial in a VA national cemetery must be made directly with the cemetery. Requests cannot be made via the Internet. The VA does not make funeral arrangements nor prepare the body for burial or cremation. Families should make these arrangments with a funeral provider or cremation office. Any item or service obtained from a funeral home or cremation office will be at the families' expense. Some veterans may also be eligible for burial allowances.

VA SERVICES

The services the VA provides for burial or inurnment of veterans in national cemeteries include:

- Opening and closing of the grave.
- Perpetual care.
- A government headstone or marker of either granite, marble, or bronze. Upright headstones in granite and marble are available. Niche markers are also available to mark columbaria.
- A burial flag.

- A Presidential Memorial Certificate.
- A military funeral honors ceremony, which includes folding and presenting the United States burial flag and the playing of Taps.

VETERANS' DEPENDENTS

Veterans' spouses and dependents may also be buried in a national cemetery. Burial benefits for spouses and dependents buried in a national cemetery include:

- Burial with the veteran.
- Perpetual care.
- The spouse's or dependents' name and date of birth and death inscribed on the veteran's headstone.
- Eligible spouses and dependents may be buried, even if they predecease the veteran.

HEADSTONES OR MARKERS

A government headstone or marker for the unmarked grave of any deceased eligible veteran in any cemetery around the world, regardless of their date of death is furnished, on request, at no charge to the applicant.

PRE-PAID SOCIETIES OR GROUP

Prepaid services are typically sold in the form of insurance policies or service agreements, which are either paid for in advance, or by regular installments. The major advantage of prepaid services is that the price is locked in with the signing of the contract. Before purchasing this kind of service, check with your financial advisor. Depending on your personal circumstances, purchasing a life insurance policy may be in your best interests.

BEGINNING THE PROCESS

Following is an example of a pre-need plan that utilizes cremation.

At death, a call begins the process. Professionally trained personnel go to the place of death to transport the deceased to a climate controlled holding facility for proper care and storage.

The organization assists in the completion of necessary documents. By law, certain forms, certificates, and authorizations must be completed before cremation can take place. In all cases, a death certificate is mandatory. Once completed, the certificate is then delivered to the physician and/or medical examiner for signatures and a statement regarding cause of death. The time it takes to obtain the signatures varies, especially if an autopsy or medical records are requested The cremation usually takes place after the necessary authorizations and documents have been properly signed and filed with the local health department.

TRANSPORT AND DISTANT DEATH ARRANGEMENTS

An additional and extra cost feature, a travel protection plan, will bring the deceased "home" from any place in the world.

AFTER CREMATION

Following cremation, ashes or cremated remains may be dispersed as directed by survivors or returned to the family.

DISCOUNT CASKET SUPPLIERS AND "GREEN" SERVICES

It's only natural that the $20 billion-a-year mortuary industry would provide fertile ground for entrepreneurs. Couple that with the urge to "go green," new opportunities abound. Green funerals are in vogue; in 45 states citizens can legally bypass funeral homes and obtain permits to handle the body on their own. Burials on private property are all but impossible in cities and require local zoning approval in rural areas. Those who want to handle the internment of family themselves should check local regulations. Asking a local funeral home executive for help is a good idea.

Businesses have been developed based on the realization that with the emotions of death, people are particularly vulnerable to overpricing and sales pressures when purchasing caskets, urns, vaults, monuments, flowers and other funeral services. The typical after-death discount service *(at very competitive prices.)* include services like:

- Selection from the same caskets that funeral homes offer. Caskets can be bronze, copper, stainless steel, cherry, mahogany, maple, oak, pecan, and more
- A large in-store inventory of caskets to choose from
- Savings of up to 75% over funeral home casket prices
- Casket prices starting at around $395
- Delivery to any funeral home

- Additional burial items, including monuments, markers, burial vaults, urns and flowers
- Clients may utilize the firm's experience *(as consultants)* when making decisions and in preparation for or arranging funeral services
- Pre-need planning of funeral services

From modest caskets to burials in tombstone-free nature preserves, green services emphasize finding a greener way to go. Going beyond the traditional provision of services, green services embrace an environmental movement that didn't exist decades ago. For example, there is some interest in conducting a funeral in the family's own home. In this mode, there is no embalming, no funeral directors, and no sticker shock. Instead, for a very small fee when compared with funeral home prices, a company will help wash, clothe, and give a wake for the departed. Or, for the real do-it-your-selfers, purchase a do-it-yourself handbook that tackles everything from how to move a body *(the expression, "dead weight" has real roots, warns the handbook)*, to how to keep it cool *(dry ice is best, but frozen peas are fine, too)*.

THE PROFESSIONAL ADVANTAGE

Some funeral directors believe their "image" needs a makeover. They have begun to offer services aimed at boomers' lifestyle and to promise mourners a more personal experience without the risk of a financial nightmare. A particular skill of the professionals is their ability to bring about ceremony and ritual in a very short period.

You need to think through the options and make your choices.

Once that's done, the next step is not as easy.

YOUR Funeral...

A short primer on a very important event

What with all the sadness and trauma going on in the world at the moment, it is worth reflecting on the death of a very important person, which almost went unnoticed.

Larry LaPrise, the man who wrote the novelty song, "The Hokey Pokey," died peacefully at age 93.

The most traumatic part for his family was getting him into the coffin. They put his left leg in, and then the trouble started.

(For those of you who don't remember the song)
You put your left leg in,
you put your left leg out.
You put your left leg in,
and you shake it all about.
You do the hokey pokey
and you turn yourself around.
That what it's all about.

THIS IS YOUR MOMENT!

Anticipating your funeral gives you the opportunity to be both Star and Director! All the work you've done to this point is in preparation for the time your friends and family get together to celebrate your life. Many will mourn your passing; others will rejoice, for they know you've gone to a heavenly place. Same will say you've gone where there is no pain, where human frailties are done away with, where the streets are paved with gold, where the golf courses are always in good shape, where you won't have to worry about cholesterol, and on and on. But there's one thing for sure: **For your time on earth, when it's over, it's over.**

Now, before it's too late, let's tackle some of the really hard issues. Let's plan your funeral *(or, perhaps you've decided to have a memorial service)*. Don't think those left behind can pull together an event celebrating your life in a day or two. It can't be done. Creating an event that will memorialize your life and contribute to the memories of those left behind takes time.

Meaningful funerals do not just happen. They are well-thought-out ceremonies that require focus and time. You should do most of the planning before you die, helped by your close friends and family members. You've been collecting things in preparation for this day. You can have the kind of funeral you want, just don't let your desires come as a surprise to those closest to you. And don't wait until you're about dead. Bringing loved ones into the loop and expending the energy to create a personalized, inclusive ceremony will help your family and other mourners for the rest of their lives.

Remember, funerals and memorial ceremonies are for survivors.

FUNERAL RIGHTS

As you plan for your funeral, you have some rules and rights:

1. You have the right to make use of a ceremony.

Your funeral/memorial ceremony does more than acknowledge the death of someone loved. It helps provide for the support of caring people. It is a way for those who love you to say, "We mourn this death and we need each other during this painful time." When a person is born, we have a ceremony. When a person gets married, we have a ceremony. When a person dies, we have a ceremony. Ceremonies are the milestones of life.

2. Plan a funeral/memorial ceremony that will meet the unique needs of your family and others who care about you.

Ceremonies are equally important if someone wants to be buried or cremated. While comfort and meaning are found in a traditional funeral/memorial ceremony, creating an event that reflects your unique personality is a privilege. Do not be afraid to add personal touches.

3. It's OK to ask friends and family members to be involved in the funeral.

For many, funerals are most meaningful when they involve people who loved the person who died. Loved ones and friends can be asked to give a reading, deliver a eulogy, play music, sing a solo, or plan some other event that will be part of the funeral. Your self-written obituary will be an important part of the service. If you want it read in addition to being in the service bulletin, let everybody know.

4. You have the freedom to decide whether your body will be viewed.

While viewing the body is not appropriate for all cultures and faiths, many find it helps them acknowledge the reality of death. It also provides a way to say good-bye to the person who died. It is a personal decision best made before your death; that failing, it becomes a family decision.

5. Your loved ones have the freedom to embrace their pain during the funeral/memorial ceremony.

The funeral may be one of the most painful and cathartic moments of life. Embracing the pain of loss and expressing it openly is not an embarrassing thing to do. Crying is not a shameful event.

6. Before your death, you have the freedom to plan a funeral/ memorial ceremony that will reflect your belief system.

Faith is a part of your life. The funeral/memorial is an ideal time for you express your faith and help others find comfort in that faith. If your belief system is expressed with alternative beliefs, plan a ceremony to reflect that belief.

7. You can expect the funeral/memorial ceremony to cause others to search for deeper meaning before, during, and after the service.

When someone loved dies, questioning the very meaning of life and death is natural.

8. Memories of the past contribute to the dignity of your life and are useful during the funeral/memorial ceremony.

Memories are one of the best legacies that exist after your death. Asking those attending to share special memories is meaningful and helpful.

9. Your passing may cause others great suffering and to experience physical and emotional crises.

Especially in the days immediately following your death, feelings of loss and sadness will probably leave many feeling fatigued. Survivors should respect what their bodies and minds are telling them. Daily rest and balanced meals will help.

10. Expect loved ones to move through their grief and heal.

While the funeral/memorial ceremony is an event, grief is not. Reconciling grief will not happen quickly. Loved ones will need to be patient and tolerant. Your death will change the lives of many forever.

FUNERAL PLANNING

(**Note**: this chapter changes back and forth from your own burial/cremation process to how you and others react to death. It's easier to understand the process (for me, anyway) doing it that way. You should be able to tell by the changing sentence structure. I hope it makes sense to you.)

This is where your advance planning skills come into play. Planning a funeral or memorial service is not easy. Making the decisions when there is no stress from death makes a very difficult task easier, but not easy. If you've been doing your homework you'll already have most of the answers to issues like these:

Visitation and viewing	Casket
Urn	Pallbearers
Flowers	Where to have the service
Order of service	Music
Special readings	Eulogies
Sermon	Graphics
Special effects	Program
Your own, unique ideas	

A TYPICAL FUNERAL SERVICE

If, in your life, you have not attended many funerals, there is probably a nagging doubt: "What happens?"

Most faiths have a standard liturgy. Most churches also have a written funeral policy that guides the celebration of a life lived. The church may also have a volunteer "funeral coordinator." Having access to a person who is familiar with the sequence of events is a big help. Use them if their services are offered.

What follows is a typical order of service in a protestant church, although each denomination has its own standard order of service:

- **Prelude** (*usually funeral music of some kind*)
- **Welcome** (*by the officiating minister; often used as an opportunity to tell others of the beliefs of the denomination*)
- **Invitation to Worship** (*a statement relating to the solemnity of the occasion and an invitation for all to participate*)
- **Hymn** (*usually sung in unison by the attendees; an alternative is special music performed by an instrumental group, choir, or soloist*)
- **Prayer** (*by the officiating minister or a visiting minister*)
- **Special music** (*can be whatever you want—I don't suggest a marching band inside the church, but outside is OK!*)
- **Old Testament Scripture** (*usually read by the person who will be delivering the major address or a visiting minister*)
- **New Testament Scripture** (*usually read by the person who will be delivering the major address or a visiting minister*)
- **Meditation or Sermon** (*by the officiating minister or by a visiting minister; is the recitation of highlights in the life of the deceased, personal recollections and spiritual exhortation regarding living a better life*)
- **Eulogies** (*decided in advance by the dead person or selected by survivors. Giving a eulogy is a significant honor and should be given considerable forethought*)
- **Special music** (*again, your choice; just use good judgment*)
- **Pastoral Prayer**
- **Affirmation of Faith** (*a statement of relevant belief of your faith, usually read in unison*)
- **Closing Hymn** (*may be performed by a group, as a solo, or sung by the attendees*)
- **Benediction** (*the blessing by the minister on those attending*)
- **Postlude** (*typically performed by an organ or piano, but could be any musical group*)

Following the service, the family receives condelences from those attending. It is increasingly popular to have a light meal or appetizers in an appropriate location. At that time friends and relatives socialize.

Within that general outline, anything else is fair game. If you choose to have a funeral that's quite unusual, check with your church, and if they frown on doing what you want, try the funeral home. They may make their chapel available to you. Failing that, rent a hall. Remember, this is your funeral.

With computers and projectors, there are a great many options that did not exist years ago. Very professional presentations that highlight specific events, family members, hopes for the future and expressions of remembrance for friends and family are now possible. In addition, there are many musical choices, including performances that reflect a specific theme.

Be careful. The message of remembrance is most important. Don't let the theme and its presentation overcome the significance of the event. There are examples that may be helpful in the chapter, "Funeral Stories."

SCRIPTURES, POEMS, READINGS, AND MUSIC

When thinking about the ceremony celebrating your own life, do you have favorite scriptures, poems, readings, or music that you want to be included in the service? Of course, I'm hoping you started thinking a long time ago about your personal ceremony, reviewed the many options available and made choices.

Does a favorite scripture come to mind? If it does, use it and any others you like. In addition to the Bible itself, there are many, many books of funeral-specific Bible verses that zero in on specific themes. Google "funeral scriptures;" you'll discover many choices.

The same is true for poems, readings, and music. If you haven't done your homework, don't depend on someone to do the research. There are way too many choices; having someone else make choices in a hurry is not fair to the departed or the survivors. Your death deserves the benefit of well-thought-out decisions.

One option that does take a lot of time is writing your own poem or reading. If your skill set includes this kind of creative effort, get after it. But start right away. It will take a lot of thought and time and several revisions. If you wish, check available materials. Search "funeral dramatic readings" for lots of options.

Of course, there's a marvelous fallback: your minister. He's probably got lists that will be invaluable in your selection process. So, if you're sweating a little as you think of all the work that has to be done, relax.

Help is on the way. Just ask.

WHAT ARE SURVIVORS EXPECTED TO SAY AND DO?

When talking to or writing to a family about the death of their loved one, finding just the right words is extremely difficult. Following are some simple phrases you can use. Believe me, whatever you say will be appreciated.

"I'm praying for you."

"I want to share your burden. Would it be helpful if I were to..."(*It is important to make a specific offer here because often a person grieving won't be capable of making a to-do list.*)

"Our Deepest Sympathy..."

"With Deepest Sympathy..."

"Our thoughts and prayers are with you."

"*(The deceased name)* was a dear friend."

"He/She lives with us in memory and will for evermore."

"The love you shared will light our way."

"The memory of you two will forever be with us."

"He/She will never be forgotten."

"His/her memory will always be in our hearts."

"His/Her greatest joy was making others happy."

And there are things that are not appropriate to say:

"Perhaps it was their time...."

"You will get over this in time...."

"I understand how you feel." (*While you could very well share similar situations, each person grieves differently.*)

"Call me if you need anything." (*A grieving person or family needs to be able to say 'yes' or 'no' to an offer of help or assistance. It might be too taxing for some to have to think of things for others to do.*)

RECEIVING LINE OR AT A VISITATION

Most of us don't have a lot of experience shaking hands and giving or receiving condolences from long lines of family, friends, acquaintances and, yes, strangers. Funerals can be awkward; there is no getting around it. They can turn the most confident persons into nervous wrecks because we just don't know what to say and do when someone we know has experienced a death. It is equally as awkward for the person/people grieving as they have to deal with their emotions and play host to family, friends, and to complete strangers.

Nonetheless, a grieving family will appreciate your show of support by taking the time to attend the visitation or service. It is not necessary to be there for the entire allotted time for the visitation, and in some cases, it may be more helpful if you pay your respects and take your leave, especially if the area is overcrowded. You may not be able to speak with the person/people grieving; just sign the guest register, writing, in addition to your name, your affiliation to the deceased. The family will appreciate it.

WHAT DO YOU SAY?

If you do talk with the person/people grieving, remember, they've been talking with a lot of people. A short statement of your sorrow is all that's needed. You could say any one of the following:

"I am so sorry."

"I want to be here for you."

"I'm praying for you."

"He/She was a good person. We were friends. He/She will be missed."

"I have never been through something like this and can only imagine your feelings right now."

"I'll check again later to see if there's anything I can do."

"It's OK if you don't feel like talking right now. I'm here whenever you are ready."

"My sympathy to you and your family."

Then give way to the next person, saying something like, "I'll be here for a while longer."

AFTER THE SERVICE IS OVER

Stay in touch. When someone you care about experiences a loss, don't believe they're OK after a week or so. Although the usual thing seems to be to send a sympathy card and then relax, there's more. While sending a card is a great thing to do, you will be most helpful when you offer to do something physical to show support, even though they may not be ready to take you up on your offer right away. The family needs a lot of things as they begin to recover from the shock of loss, but the timing varies from person to person. Don't assume sending a card ends your participation in the recovery process. There are many things you could do after the burial. Here are a few suggestions:

- Send flowers to brighten their day
- Give them a call; they'll tell you if it is a good time or not
- Offer to prepare a meal or take them to dinner
- Help with the housework or house sit to give them some time to themselves
- Invite them to go out with you

Don't expect the survivors to be their old selves any time soon. It will take time, so don't expect too much when you offer your help. The main thing is your offer. It helps them by knowing they have friends who are concerned and are offering their support.

THANK YOU CARD ETIQUETTE

As a person who has lost a loved one, you're grieving. Your friends need to know you are aware of and appreciate their concern for you. There's just so much others can do to help. It will help a lot when you acknowledge their generosity. Just the thought of the passage of a friend or loved one is terrifying. At this point in your life, it's hard to think about thanking others for their care. However, it is appropriate to express your thanks to those who lent their support, and you can't wait too long before you do. Do it. You'll be glad you did.

Thank you cards should be sent to:

- People who sent flowers and or sympathy cards
- People who made donations to your specified charity
- People who donated personal services (*transportation, baby-sitting, etc.*) or food

- Pallbearers
- Friends
- Neighbors
- Relatives
- Others who performed special tasks or came from a long distance

There are cards designed specifically for thanking others. The funeral home and stationers sell preprinted thank you cards that are particularly appropriate. If you can, try to personalize the card by adding a sentence or two in addition to the pre-printed copy. You could write in your own handwriting a sentence like:

"The flower arrangement you sent was lovely; thank you"
"We really appreciate your help during this sad time; thank you so much"
"Your care meant so much; thanks for your concern."

Sending a thank you email just doesn't seem right for this situation. However, you might want to put a general thank you notice in the newspaper. A public notice is often a way to thank hospital staff, care giver(s), the funeral home and staff, any catering or transportation services. (*However, I personally doubt people look for a "thank you" in the newspaper.*) If pressed, you can include in your newspaper announcement friends and associates who sent cards, flowers and made donations to specified charities. But this group should also receive an individual note. Don't let too much time go by before you send your note. Use a three-week rule; send your acknowledgment before three weeks go by.

STRESS

Families that have suffered loss have experienced:

- Increased irritability, arguments, and family discord, including domestic violence
- Clinging, acting out and regressive behavior by children
- Illness and psychosomatic problems for adults and children
- Exhaustion
- Decreased intimacy
- Increased alcohol consumption and/or substance abuse
- Survivor's guilt

WHAT YOU CAN DO FOR FAMILY MEMBERS:

- Listen and empathize. A sympathetic listener is important.
- Spend time with the traumatized person. There is no substitute for personal presence.
- Offer assistance and sympathy. Voiced support is critical.
- Re-assure children, the elderly and even adults: they are safe.
- Don't tell traumatized people that they are "lucky it wasn't worse." Such statements do not console traumatized people.
- Tell them, instead, that you're sorry such an event has occurred, and that you want to understand and assist them.
- Respect a family member's need for privacy and private grief.

WHAT YOU CAN DO FOR YOURSELF:

- Exercise. Physical exercise can help relieve stress. Strenuous exercise alternated with relaxation will help alleviate physical reactions.
- Remember that you're experiencing normal reactions to an abnormal situation.
- Talk to people. Talk is healing medicine.
- Accept support from loved ones, friends, and neighbors. People do care.
- Give yourself permission to feel rotten. You're suffering from loss. It's OK to grieve for the loss of material things.
- When you're feeling rotten, remember those around you are also under stress.
- Don't make any big life changes immediately. During periods of extreme stress, we all tend to make misjudgments.
- Eat well-balanced, regular meals and get plenty of rest.
- Be kind to yourself.

Funeral Stories...

Learn from the experiences of others

People were sitting in their pews talking. Suddenly, Satan appeared at the front of the church. Everyone started screaming and running for the front entrance, trampling each other in a frantic effort to get away from the evil incarnate. Soon, everyone had exited the church except for one elderly gentleman, who sat calmly in his pew, seemingly oblivious to the fact that God's ultimate enemy was in his presence.

Satan walked up to the old man and said, "Don't you know who I am?"

The old man replied, "Yep, sure do."

"Aren't you afraid of me?" Satan asked.

"Nope, sure ain't," replied the old man.

"Don't you realize I could kill you with a word?" asked Satan.

"Don't doubt it for a minute," replied the old man.

"Don't you know I could cause you profound, horrifying agony for all eternity?" persisted Satan.

"Yep," was the calm reply.

"And you're not afraid of me?" asked Satan.

"Nope," was the reply.

More than a little perturbed, Satan asked, "Well, why aren't you afraid of me?"

The old man calmly replied, "Been married to your sister for 48 years."

The stories in this chapter illustrate the uniqueness of a service honoring a loved one. It is a very important event, which can be personalized in many different and loving ways. In the planning of a service, there is an opportunity to reflect on the life of the deceased and share with others how our own lives were affected by both his living and dying.

In addition to the actual formal funeral or memorial service, there is the physical part, the preparation and actual "making it happen" functions—mind boggling responsibilities.

If you don't do it before you die, someone has to be responsible for arranging for the events in the following short list (*and there are many more items not listed*):

- Burial in a cemetery, columbarium or mausoleum
- Choosing a crematory
- Choosing casket or urn
- Selecting a vault in which to place the casket
- Selecting a headstone and having it engraved
- Selecting favorite musical numbers and scriptures or readings
- Choosing musicians
- Placement of flowers in the service facility
- The graveside ceremony
- Planning of events preceding the service and after the service
- Arranging for overnight accommodations for out-of-town guest
- Seating arrangements for family and out-of-town guests
- Choosing pallbearers and honorary pallbearers
- Acquisition of photographs and mementos
- Displaying objects
- Transportation to the ceremonial site, cemetery, and home
- And many other actions

All these items must be completed before or after the service event itself.

It's a big job, a very pressure-packed responsibility, especially if it has to be done at the last moment. Those who have done it after the death of a loved one attest to the value of advance planning.

Though seldom referred to as "theater," quite often, in addition to the words of the minister, the other things that are done contribute substantially to making the celebration event one that touches the hearts of many. The stories that follow illustrate the way other families have put together the activities to create an atmosphere that reflects the personality of the deceased.

The words of survivors you'll be reading haven't been changed. The authors are sharing their very personal story. You'll not be able to deny the creativity and thought involved. None of the funerals are "plain vanilla;" you'll have to decide for yourself whether the descriptions of events gave you ideas you hadn't had before, and that, perhaps, you can use.

Stories help. Knowing what someone else has done makes preparing your own funeral service easier. Deciding in advance what you want done will be a great help to your survivors.

As you plan your own funeral, take any of the ideas from the stories and make them your own. Maybe reading them will trigger other, original ideas. Remember the words from Chapter 17, "Your Funeral?" "Anticipating your funeral gives you the opportunity to be both Star and Director!" In your advance planning, do what you think appropriate to add purpose and meaning to your ceremony. A funeral is an important event; you can make yours an occasion different from all others and one that impacts positively on friends and relatives.

SOME VERY PERSONAL FUNERAL STORIES

There are four funeral stories in this chapter, the titles of which are listed below. Each presents a different perspective to the commemoration of a loved one's life.

The "Hunting" Funeral

My War Hero's Funeral

Celebrating My Wife's Faith

Kate, My Guardian Angel

THE "HUNTING" FUNERAL

Dennis was the outdoorsy sibling. Our dad had hunted ducks since his childhood, and found a willing pupil in Dennis. I lasted through three duck seasons, but finally worked up the courage to tell my dad that I just didn't like getting up at five in the morning in order to go sit in a freezing cold duck blind. So, while I went the way of baseball and soccer, Dennis went the way of hunting, fishing, and any other activity that took him onto water or into the woods.

Both Dennis and I stuck around our hometown. I got married and had two kids, while Dennis was still dating the same woman, Diane, after 10 years.

Dennis had become one of the most recognizable guys in town. He stumbled into selling insurance, and turned out to have the selling instinct with a great personality. He lined his insurance office with stuffed trophies and game fish. He had even gone Marlin fishing and had a 300-pound Marlin on the wall.

Dennis dressed almost the same every day: blue jeans, plaid, long-sleeve shirt with the sleeves rolled up to the elbow, and a ball cap (although the ball caps changed almost daily because he had one with every logo imaginable). He was a fixture around town with his black or red pick-up trucks (yeah, he had two), and was almost never seen without his two chocolate brown lab dogs peeking over the sidewalls of the bed of the truck. People driving other cars would give a little wave as they passed Dennis. His truck would often be pulled up alongside the curb, and Dennis would be out on the sidewalk, talking to two or three people at a time.

I still dream about getting that phone call. Mom called to tell me Dennis had been accidentally killed by a semi-truck that crossed the center line because the driver was both drunk and tired. Both of the dogs were killed too.

Mom, dad, Diane, and I needed to have a funeral for Dennis but almost didn't know where to begin. We made sure to include Diane because as far as we were concerned, she was practically Dennis's wife. But she certainly didn't have her own financial resources to provide a funeral for Dennis. Dennis had sold our funeral director all of his personal and business insurance, and that made us realize how many people's lives had been touched by Dennis. Our local funeral director helped us to create a funeral ceremony for Dennis that would be meaningful to almost an entire town.

The funeral director surprised us by telling us Dennis had taken out a special life insurance policy on himself that was specifically designed to pay for his funeral. In reality, we shouldn't have been surprised that Dennis, because of his career, had planned ahead and had used insurance to make sure his funeral was paid for. By buying the insurance, Dennis was protecting my mom and dad from any financial burden.

We decided that Dennis was known as a personality, but also known by the comfort he brought by being so visible in the community. So, we dressed Dennis in his favorite clothes — blue jeans, plaid shirt, with the sleeves rolled up. I chose the pair of blue jeans he would wear, mom chose the shirt, and dad picked out the ball cap.

We chose a casket made of stainless steel painted in the color, Hunter Green. The vault we chose was one that sealed and was in the middle price range.

We continued on with the outdoors/hunter/fisherman theme. We chose to have memorial folders printed with Dennis's picture on the front showing him pheasant hunting with his two dogs. These were handed out at the visitation and at the funeral. We had the image of a fisherman printed on the front of the thank you cards that we sent to everyone after the funeral. On the cover of the register book, we had the image of a picture–perfect lake shore with trees and small hills in the background.

We took the extra step of mentioning this "theme" in Dennis's obituary and encouraging anyone to bring in pictures, flowers, small mementoes or gifts related to Dennis and to his outdoor lifestyle, all of which we displayed during the 3-hour visitation the night before the funeral. We also brought in our own pictures and mementoes to be displayed. These included Dennis's fishing rods, guns, decoys and duck calls. We also brought in a sampling of the trophies from his insurance office, and other items that would conjure up wonderful memories of Dennis.

At the funeral the next day, after everyone was seated in the church pews (plus many people standing along the side aisles and in the back of the church), we began playing a video tribute of Dennis on a large screen positioned on the altar of the church. The song played throughout the video was "Memories," sung by Elvis Presley. To tell Dennis's life story, the funeral director had taken the pictures we had supplied that showed Dennis from the time he was a baby through all the other milestones of his life, and put them altogether in a video sequence that drew upon the words of the song. When it was done, everyone broke out in a long-sustained applause. The video had done what the funeral director said it would do, draw everyone together in our time of sorrow.

After the song, the minister reminded us of the Bible scripture that could help us reflect upon the death of someone so close to us.

Then, he invited people to stand up and share a story about Dennis. As it turned out, the stories were all hilarious. That church was just roaring with laughter for about 15 minutes as different people shared stories that none of us had ever heard before, nor most of the congregation, for that matter. It was a disappointment that the stories had to stop, but the time turned out to be a wonderful reflection for all of us.

Diane wrote a 'goodbye' letter to Dennis, and had previously shared it with us. We thought it so moving and beautiful we asked her to read it at the funeral. She reluctantly agreed but only if my wife would join her at the lectern for support. Diane made it to the lectern, but as she *completed the first sentence, her voice cracked, stressed from the emotion she was experiencing. She handed the letter to my wife. My wife understood and began reading the soulful words of Diane. As my wife read, Diane began crying so hard I, along with everyone else in the church, were now crying too. My wife pulled Diane next to her and hugged her, and continued to hug her as she continued reading.*

Diane then asked that the song be played that was on the radio in the truck cab that night some 10 years ago, lit only by the glow of the dashboard lights, when Dennis and Diane shared their first kiss. That song was "Still," by Lionel Ritchie.

We concluded the funeral ceremony by playing a song that Dennis had told me, when we were just teenagers, 'talked to him.' He never elaborated on that point, and I never asked any more about it, but I made sure it was played at this funeral. So, as the song played, "Don't Let The Sun Go Down On Me," sung by Elton John, I and the other casket bearers escorted the casket down the church aisle and then lifted the casket into the hearse waiting a the bottom of the church steps.

The cemetery procession was a special event for all of us. We used Dennis's other truck to lead the procession while pulling Dennis's bass boat. And, mysteriously, in the back of the truck were two identical chocolate lab dogs. At first, the sight of the two dogs took our breath away –it was almost like seeing ghosts. We found out at the cemetery that two of Dennis's hunting buddies each had a chocolate lab and they put them in the back of the truck because the truck just wouldn't look right going down the road without those two dog's ears splayed back from the wind. We loved this small gesture of love. On our way to the cemetery, we directed the procession to drive right through downtown, since Dennis had sold most of those business owners their insurance. Many of the stores' employees came out on the sidewalk and paid silent homage to my brother as his hearse passed by.

At the cemetery, as the casket bearers, we removed the casket from the hearse and placed the casket on the temporary stand so the casket was positioned above the grave where the bottom part of the vault had already been installed.

We had chosen a long-time friend of my mom to officiate at the funeral, and she read a short poem. Then, the funeral director opened the casket and helped Diane place a fishing rod and a shotgun in the casket with Dennis. She placed her hand upon Dennis's hand, leaned over, and gently kissed his check. Almost the entire crowd began to cry with her as they sensed how deep her loss really was. As the casket was lowered, everyone was invited to throw a flower onto the casket as their final gesture of goodbye.

My mom and dad, my wife, Diane and I formed a tight circle, with each of us having our arms around the shoulders of the person standing next to us. We all broke down in tears and cried as we heard the casket being slowly lowered into the grave. Still embracing each other, we formed a line and watched as the funeral director and his staff helped to slide the heavy vault lid over the base of the vault and lower it into place, to be permanently sealed.

What had everyone wondering was the open grave right next to Dennis's grave. My dad and I walked to the back of Dennis pickup truck, pulled down the rear gate. There were two smaller sized caskets, one for each of Dennis's dogs that had been killed on that terrible night. Yes, the dogs were in the caskets. We had obtained special permission from the cemetery to allow the dogs to be buried with Dennis. (It helped that Dennis had sold the cemetery its property and liability insurance coverage.) My dad took one and I took one; we brought them to the side of the grave. With the help of two of our friends, we used ropes to lower the two caskets down into the grave next to Dennis.

Our family each took a shovel and placed a shovel full of dirt on top of Dennis's vault, and another shovel full on the dogs' two caskets. Just at that moment, the two chocolate labs that had been riding in the back of Dennis's pickup truck began to howl. It was that mournful howl that you remember hearing in the distance when you're not quite sure whether a dog has been hurt, or is truly sad. It made us laugh and cry at the same time, realizing that those two dogs probably knew exactly what was going on.

MY WAR HERO'S FUNERAL

John, my husband, had served in the Navy during WWII. He served on a ship that had been sunk by a German U-boat. John was one of the survivors who had managed to get off the ship as it was sinking. He had waited in the water for over 36 hours for his rescue.

Almost 400 men with life preservers on had gone into the water that late Friday afternoon. They formed circles, and tied themselves together to help ensure that no one got swept away by waves or currents. John had said the worst fear was not knowing what was beneath them. They worried about sharks, and even saw a couple.

Although a distress call had gone out, no other ships could get them until the other German U-boats were destroyed. They were never able to determine if the U-boat that had sunk John's ship was later destroyed or not.

I met John just after he had returned from his tour of duty. We fell in love almost immediately, and we were married just six months later.

John was particularly proud of having been able to serve his country during WWII. He remained in touch with several of his buddies he had met on the ship. They wrote to each other, called, and every once in awhile, one of them would stop by and visit if he was in the area on business or a vacation trip. We would often schedule our vacation trips so that we could drive through a town where one of John's navy buddies lived.

John was also an active member in our local VFW, and enjoyed marching in the area parades in his full dress uniform (which still fit him after all those years). John seemed able to seek out those men in a crowd that were about his age, and strike up a conversation that inevitably led to talking about each other's service in WWII. They shared stories of combat, but more often stories about being in the Navy or Army or Marines, and the strong, unbreakable friendships that arose from that experience. John died the day after the 4th of July, one of his favorite days of the year. Even though John was 75, I was still shocked by his death. Partly because it just came out of the blue, with no warning. John died of a heart attack while at the local grocery store. I was at my bridge club and John was busying himself running errands. Although the ambulance was called, he apparently was already dead by the time the paramedics arrived.

Just six years earlier, while watching TV, John and I had seen a commercial about buying life insurance that would be used to pay for funeral expenses. We certainly weren't well off financially. John's pension plus social security got us by only because our house was fully paid for. So, we had decided to make the monthly payments on a small life insurance policy, one for each of us, just to make sure neither of us was left with any financial hardship from paying for a funeral.

Our only son, David, and his family came from California as soon as I called to tell them about John. Just as we were about to head out the door to go to the funeral home, David called me onto the back porch and told me that he would help with the funeral finances. I started to cry and I hugged him. I told him about the life insurance policies and reassured him that his mom would be just fine.

John and I had been to a couple of the funerals of other members of the VFW in recent years, so I already knew about some of the special and meaningful things that could be done for someone who had served in the armed forces. I told this to our funeral director and we proceeded to create a funeral that reflected John's pride in his service to his country.

My son and I picked out a wood casket because John and I had decided that we both wanted to be cremated. We picked a beautiful solid maple casket partly because there was also a solid maple cremation urn and we wanted the two to be of the same kind of wood. The urn bears the engraved image of a soldier saluting, and with the cremation urn comes a smaller memento urn, with the same engraving that would also contain a portion of John's ashes that our son David could keep. Also, the casket had space *for engravings on each of the four corners, so we selected the colored engraving of an American flag to be on each of the corners.*

We arranged to have a 3-hour visitation the night before the funeral at the funeral home, with a viewing of John. The unopened half of John's casket was draped with a full sized American flag. We also displayed the American P.O.W. (Prisoner of War) flag. John had also devoted some of his time to raising money to aid in the search for missing P.O.W.'s.

The funeral director set up a table, which he called the memory table, to hold mementos of John's life. David and I searched the house for small items that reminded us of different parts of John's life. We looked, too, for remembrances of significant events that played a role in all of our lives. We took those items in to set on the memory table. We also had called many of John's closest friends and asked them to share mementos or pictures too.

It was amazing how many people were drawn to these objects and pictures during the visitation. Someone would pick up an item and tell me a story that it reminded them of. It turned out we were told many stories that involved John we had never heard before.

The funeral was actually held at the V.F.W. hall. At the funeral, we had five of John's closest friends and David act as casket bearers. We also named another 20 people, John's closest friends, as honorary casket bearers. All of them sat together at the front of the hall in recognition of their role at the funeral.

With John's casket sitting at the front of the hall, with at least 50 American flags lining all four walls of the hall, we started the funeral by playing one of John's favorite songs, "God Bless the U.S.A.," sung by Lee Greenwood. We had passed out pamphlets with the words of the song, and we asked the entire audience to join in and sing along with the song, which they did.

David had asked to say a few words at the funeral. David spoke proudly of the role his father had played in his life, and how he now saw many of his father's traits and reheard many of his father's words coming from his mouth as he raised two sons of his own.

I had also asked one of John's closest friends, Cal, who had served on the ship with him, and had also been one of the survivors of that ship's sinking, to speak at the funeral. I specifically asked Cal to share the story of that day on the ship and how it had shaped the course of his life. I told him I was asking him to do it because I wanted those attending to get a sense of how that same event had shaped John's life, and was something that was with him every day for the rest of his life.

Cal began the story of that ship's sinking, but when he came to the part where the ship was struck by two torpedoes, he began to cry. It was clear that reliving this event was difficult for Cal, and not only because one his best friends had just died. I heard something as Cal spoke that I hadn't anticipated—it was as if I was hearing the story for the first time. It turns out John had "overlooked" some facts when he had recalled the story over the many years of his life. John had, in fact, saved Cal's life, and the lives of many other men on board that fateful ship. They were below deck when the torpedoes had hit. It was John who carried two unconscious men (one of them Cal) up two flights of stairs to the main deck where they regained consciousness and could get away from the sinking ship on their own. It was also John, who, before going up those stairs, had closed a watertight hatch door that had provided critical time for others to escape the sinking ship before it went under.

I began to cry. I had never heard this part of the story before. I hadn't realized how brave my John had been. I stood up and I walked up to Cal and hugged him and we cried together. David later told me that everyone had began to cry as I stood there hugging Cal. After we had somewhat composed ourselves, Cal escorted me back to my seat, and the funeral continued.

I ended the funeral by playing a song that had meant a lot to both John and me, "I'll be Seeing You:" sung by Tony Bennett. As the song played, our funeral director presented me with the flag that had been draped over John's casket. The flag was folded into a triangle, which is the formal military style of folding a flag when it is removed from flying on a flagpole. I purchased a triangular-shaped oak box, with a glass front, to put the flag in and now it hangs on the wall of my living room.

As the song continued, the funeral directors came forward and rolled John's casket down the aisle and out the door to the hearse waiting at the curb. They were led by a color guard of other V.F.W. members.

After John's casket was placed in the hearse, a rifle guard composed of even more members of the V.F.W. fired a three-shot volley into the air. After the last shot, there was silence. Then, from the distance, we heard a bugler play Taps for John.

CELEBRATING MY WIFE'S FAITH

Kathy was a wonderful woman, wife and mother. She also had a very strong belief in her Catholic faith. She had found her strength in her faith when she was just nineteen. Both of her parents were killed in a car accident, and she was left to care for two younger siblings, ages 16 and 13. Faced with a lack of money, she, her brother, and her sister all worked to put food on the table and clothes on their backs. Her aunts and uncles offered little help since they were financially strapped themselves, with their own children to feed. But Kathy and her siblings were determined to make it on their own.

Times were tough, and the little money they made was spent just to keep them alive.

Kathy never really had quite understood what it was that God, through the Catholic Church, was doing for her, until in her desperation for guidance she decided to pray for relief from the burdens she faced. She had told me she had gone to the church late in the afternoon and walked in, but no one was around. She walked down the aisle and knelt at the prayer rail. She said she had tried praying silently, hearing the words only in her mind. But, then something told her to pray out loud, which she did. She decided not to ask God for anything, but instead, tell God her story, what she was faced with.

As she concluded, she said she felt a sense of relief pass through her and she knew it was God preparing her to have the energy and the courage to go on. Walking out the church, she turned to her right and walked right into me. She fell to the ground and I picked her up.

Yes, I think it was love at first sight, and certainly God's providence.

We almost never missed Mass after that, and always went together.

Just six months after bumping into each other, we were married in that very church. One of the few times we missed going to Mass was because she was giving birth to our son, Matthew. Otherwise, you could find us at church participating in all of the various functions the church was involved in helping its parishioners to help others.

Then, later, as Kathy lay in her hospital bed, the doctors had given our children and me the bad news. The cancer was now so widespread in her body that it would be just a matter of hours or days before she died. Kathy had waited too long to tell me about the pain she was having, and by the time I convinced her to go and see a doctor, the cancer was so widespread any type of aggressive form of treatment would have been fatal, let alone the cancer itself.

I asked the hospital to call Father Mike to give him the news. I was worried I wouldn't be able to keep my composure to have a phone conversation. About an hour later, Father Mike came. Kathy recognized him and knew why he was there. Kathy's only words to him were, "Pray for me one last time." Father Mike conducted the Last Rites and did pray for Kathy. In fact, all of us held hands in a semicircle around the bed, with Kathy herself completing the circle and prayed.

Kathy went into God's hands that very night.

Initially, Father Mike joined the kids and me at the funeral home to make arrangements. He wanted to make it easy for the funeral director to schedule a time for the burial mass, and he could confirm the time with him. I was also glad Father Mike was there, because there were a couple of unique things I had planned for Kathy's visitation and funeral and wanted to make sure it was OK with him and that it was OK with the church. Father Mike was 20 years younger than I was and he completely under stood and agreed with everything I wanted to do.

Kathy and I had talked about being cremated, so I wanted to follow through with her expectations. We had both talked about the fact that we wanted to have a visitation the night before the funeral, so we did that.

The next day, the funeral actually began at the funeral home. We said prayers and our final farewell, and then, with the hearse, we formed a procession and traveled the twelve blocks to the Catholic Church.

More distant family members and friends were already seated on both sides of the aisle as the casket bearers carried the casket to the back of the chapel and set the casket on a wheeled casket bier.

The funeral liturgy began there with the absolution of the casket.

Then, my children and I were presented with the casket pall to place over the entire casket as the Priest spoke the words "... on the day of your Baptism you put on Christ." At that point, we played the song, "Ave Maria," sung by Perry Como. Kathy and I loved to hear that song. Father Mike and the servers began the processional down the aisle toward the front of the church while the song played.

Following them were the funeral directors pushing the casket on its wheeled bier, followed by the casket bearers, and then me and my children.

At the close of the Mass, the church hymn, "Panis angelicus," was played.

Father Mike joined with the congregation after the Mass for the Final Commendation. Then, Father Mike led the processional back down the aisle. My children removed the Pall from the casket; the casket bearers picked up the casket, carried it down the church steps, and placed it in the hearse.

The next day our funeral director stopped by our house with the cremation urn engraved with Kathy's name and dates of birth and death. I placed the urn in the bay window of our kitchen.

KATE, MY GUARDIAN ANGEL

My sister Kate was just 11 months older than I. And, with no other brothers or sisters, we were almost inseparable as we grew up. One day, when we were about 7 years old, we overheard our mom telling someone that she felt her guardian angel helped her. That night, as we were going to bed in the bedroom we shared, Kate asked my mom what a guardian angel was. After my mom explained it, she told us we each had our own guardian angel.

From that time on, we believed in our guardian angel, and sometimes even talked to her. (We just assumed that girls had girl guardian angels and vice versa). Many times we talked about how events that evolved in front of us simply must have been guided by the guardian angel. Why else could things have turned out so wonderfully?

In our teens, the concept of guardian angels just faded out of our minds. But Kate and I remained inseparable, even through college.

The years passed, but our bond held strong even though Kate lived in the big city that was about 3 hours from where I lived.

Then, at Kate's 50th birthday party, Kate took me aside in her bedroom and told me she had been diagnosed earlier that week with cancer. We both sat beside each other on her bed and cried together.

This was a battle Kate wanted to fight, but she worried about her ability to conjure up the energy to beat the cancer. I got down on my knees next to the bed to pray with my arms perched on top of the bed, just like I did when I was a little girl. Without a word, Kate knelt beside me and she listened as I began to pray for her. In my prayer, I called upon Kate's guardian angel to remember who Kate was and to give her the strength and guidance to fight the cancer.

Eleven months later, Kate's cancer was nowhere to be found in her body. And both Kate's and my belief in our respective guardian angels was renewed. After that, we talked about our guardian angels often, seeing how they were guiding us through many of life's tough decisions at the times when you are forced to make a choice that will change the course of your life.

Fourteen years later, Kate died quietly in her sleep when a small artery ruptured in her brain. I remember when the phone call came. It was just after 2:00 a.m. I knew when I awakened from the phone ringing, it was about Kate because I had just been dreaming about her.

Kate's husband, Bill, and their kids invited me to participate in the funeral arrangements. I was glad they gave me that opportunity. It turns out that Kate and Bill had purchased insurance to pay for their funerals, so I was glad to know the cost of the funeral would not be a financial burden on their family. After Kate's bout with cancer, she and Bill had decided that some financial planning was in order, and added this type of insurance to help them.

I told the funeral director about the guardian angels that Kate and I shared, and Kate's kids shared their own stories about how their mom talked about the guardian angel that had helped her win her fight against cancer. The funeral director suggested we make Kate's belief in her guardian angel a central part of the funeral we would have.

Kate had always expressed a desire to be cremated, but she had also said that she wanted a funeral because she understood the importance the ceremony played in helping people in their process of grieving. When our grandmother had died when I was nine and Kate was 10, Kate and I had not been allowed to go to the visitation or attend the funeral. We were told "...that was not a place for children." Well, that had always troubled Kate because it was as if Grandma had just disappeared. Kate wanted to make sure that never happened to any other children in our family, and she felt that a visitation, with an open casket, was particularly important to allow everyone to start their own mental process of understanding death and to begin dealing with their grief.

Kate's husband picked a beautiful solid maple casket. He picked maple because their whole yard is filled with big, beautiful maple trees. He selected an urn that was also made of solid maple.

We began making Kate's funeral meaningful to us by not writing the traditional, boring obituary. We took the time to write about Kate's life–the good and the bad. And, we took several paragraphs to describe Kate's belief in her guardian angel and how that angel would be part of the funeral her family and friends were about to attend. In the obituary, we asked friends to make angels part of their gifts to the family by having them donate money to a charity named "Guardian Angels" that funds special surgical procedures for children living in poverty that have physical deformities.

At the visitation, we asked the children attending to draw pictures of angels to give to Kate. The funeral home took the colored pictures and made color photocopies of them for us to keep as a keepsake. Then, our funeral director helped each child place their angel picture in the casket with Kate. It was their special way of saying goodbye, and giving Kate angels to carry her to heaven.

As Kate lay in her casket, we selected a small broach pin, in the form of an angel, to be pinned to Kate's blouse. The funeral director told us he would remove the pin just before Kate was cremated and would return the pin to Kate's husband as a keepsake. Ultimately, Bill placed the pin next to Kate's urn on a shelf in his house.

At the start of the ceremony, as Kate's casket was rolled down the aisle to the front of the altar, we played the song, "On Angels' Wings," sung by a soloist who was standing in the balcony at the back of the chapel.

Toward the end of the ceremony, we played another song, "Wind Beneath My Wings," sung by Bette Midler. Kate and I had talked many *times about that song, and how it applied to each one of us, having helped each of us during some of the tough times our lives.*

At the end of the ceremony, I went to the front of the chapel. There we had arranged to have a small bell mounted on a stand. I turned to the audience and asked them to come forward as they left the chapel to ring the bell just once. I reminded them of the story we had learned in Sunday school as children, when our teacher told us that every time a bell rings an angel gets its wings, and this was our chance to ensure that Kate got her wings. That brought a small, understanding laugh from the audience. But, one by one, they filed out of the church pews and came forward and, with the small wooden mallet I provided to them, struck the bell once. Everyone else sat in silence as the bell tolled. Later, people told me partici-pating in Kate's funeral that way had meant an awfully lot to them.

The casket bearers then followed Kate's casket to the front door of the church. The funeral director had the casket bearers lift the casket and place it into the waiting hearse. The hearse took Kate's body to the crema-tory to begin the cremation process.

As I stood on the sidewalk and watched the hearse go down the block and turn to the right and out of sight, I felt a tug at the bottom of my dress. When I looked down, there was Kate's son's son, my great nephew, Nick, all of 6 years old. He looked up to me and said, "Did you know that Auntie Kate is going to be my guardian angel now?" I started to cry as I knelt down to hug Nick, and I whispered in his ear, "Tell her hello and I love her when you talk to her. OK?" With a great smile of satisfac-tion he said, "Sure, not a problem" as he walked away to find his dad.

The next day, we went back to the funeral home to receive the urn with Kate's cremated ashes in it. When we were there, we discovered that we could buy a small heart shaped pendant that could hold a very small amount of cremated ashes that could be kept as a keepsake. I asked Bill if he would mind if I bought the pendant and had some of Kate's ashes placed in it. Bill thought that was a great idea, and the funeral director added Kate's cremated ashes to the pendant and handed it to me. I never felt right about wearing the pendant around my neck, so I didn't. Instead, I hung the heart shaped pendant on a small display that I put in my living room.

That night, as I lay in bed reliving the events of Kate's funeral over and over, I started worrying that I wasn't falling asleep. I thought to myself 'you have to let go, Kate is in good hands.' I thought for a moment and then said a silent prayer to my guardian angel, asking her to check in on Kate from time to time, and then I drifted off to sleep.

(Various mortuaries and casket manufacturers were the sources for these stories.)

*There **is** a morning*
after the most difficult day
of your life . . . .

How do Survivors... Survive?

It's not easy, but they do

John the farmer was in the fertilized egg business. He had several hundred young layers (hens), called "pullets" and eight or ten roosters, whose job it was to fertilize the eggs.

The farmer kept records and any rooster that didn't perform went into the soup pot and was replaced. That took an awful lot of his time, so he bought a set of tiny bells and attached them to his roosters. Each bell had a different tone, so John could tell from a distance which rooster was performing.

Now he could sit on the porch and fill out an efficiency report simply by listening to the bells. The farmer's favorite rooster was old Butch, and a very fine specimen he was, too.

But on this particular morning John noticed old Butch's bell hadn't rung at all! John went to investigate. The other roosters were chasing pullets, bells-a-ringing. The pullets, hearing the roosters coming, would run for cover.

But to Farmer John's amazement, Butch had his bell in his beak, so it couldn't ring. He'd sneak up on a pullet, do his job and walk on to the next one.

John was so proud of Butch, he entered him in the Renfrew County Fair and Butch became an overnight sensation among the judges.

The result...The judges not only awarded Butch the No Bell Piece Prize but they also awarded him the Pullet Surprise as well.

Clearly Butch was a politician in the making. Who else but a politician could figure out how to win two of the most highly coveted awards on our planet by being the best at sneaking up on the populace and screwing them when they weren't paying attention?

YOU'RE A SURIVOR

You're all alone. It's not all over. It's not the end of the line. Your life will continue on, even though right now you don't think that's possible. You've never balanced a checkbook? You've never grocery shopped? You've never bought birthday or Christmas presents for the family? You've never changed the oil in the car? You've never made a Martini? Never chosen the wine at dinner?

But you're smart. You were smart enough to choose the best possible companion in the world. You were smart enough to get out of the way when it was time to replace a light bulb, repair the seam in a pair of pants, or mow the lawn.

You can get through this. You can.

The family has returned to living their lives. Friends have gone home. Neighbors are no longer bringing you food. Time to try to get back to a normal life, although you're not sure it can be done.

It can.

As the survivor, life has now taken on a wholly different perspective. What used to be done by your other half or as a pair is now done by you or hired done. Your friends will tell you your new single status will change your way of looking at facts. They're right. What used to get no thought at all now becomes an item of primary importance *(like putting together the income tax records)*.

You never worried about eating alone in a restaurant. You always had a companion to make conversation, to help decide what to order and to help eat the stuff that left with you in a "take out" box.

I haven't even dented the surface of things that are different now. I can't imagine how you feel or how things have changed for you. No one can.

But one morning you will wake up and things will be different. Not in a major way, but just a little different. This almost imperceptible difference is the beginning of healing. It's God's gift: the passage of time.

It may happen as you sit at the kitchen table, reading the morning paper and having a second cup of coffee. It's no big thing. It's nothing more than the recognition that bad things do happen to good people. The death of your loved one was not your fault. You need to get on with your life.

Recovery has begun.

HEALING

You ask yourself a very practical question: "What am I going to do?" You don't have to have a snappy answer, just say to yourself, "I've lost the person that meant the most to me; we'll never be together again. What am I going to do?"

You've recognized healing is possible. It will take a while, but do believe you will recover from this terrible loss. Healing is irregular; some days are better than others but it's ongoing. It may take a long, long time, but you will have a life, a life that will be whatever you want it to be.

You *can* move away from focusing on the death of your partner to begin to remember the good times you two shared, as well as the little things that made you happy.

Healing has begun when you can plan ahead, even if it's just a day or two, and take a positive action like making a reservation at a restaurant.

How long does it take to get to this point? It's different for everybody. The thing that is universal in the process is the recognition, finally, that healing does occur. It's not an instant thing, and there will be setbacks. Real healing begins when you're able to recognize you're having a bad day, but tomorrow will be better. It's like "bouncing back" from a setback. When you do that and understand what's happening, you're on your way to another chapter in your life.

Those of us who believe in God believe God is part of the healing process. We accept that God may be working in our life at a different pace than we'd like. We also accept that God wants the very best for us. The result of God and you working together is a NEW you. Your life will, in all likelihood, be different than it was before.

CELEBRATE THE MEMORY OF A LOVED ONE

Getting on with your life doesn't mean forgetting your loved one. It means being able to remember without falling apart. Why not do something that will be a memorial to your loved one?

Plant a tree
Make a donation in their memory
Set up a scholarship fund (*You may want to ask others to also contribute; that way a greater good can be accomplished.*)

Have a Memorial Golf Tournament
Do something very personal for yourself each year on the anniversary of the death

With your involvement in events like these, the passage of time, and the development of new interests, your grief will begin to fade. How long will it take? Probably longer than you thought. The restoration of life processes doesn't happen on a schedule that can be controlled. It takes as long as it takes. But, day by day, you will re-enter the world.

Here's something you might want to consider: Talk to your loved one's spirit. You know, have a conversation. Bring them up to date on your life. Many others have said that having a conversation like this is healing. For sure, you will be sharing an adventure.

Will your life ever be the same? No. However, a new normalcy is possible, one that is defined differently than the one you had before. You won't forget. You will still grieve, but your life will not be dominated by grief.

Your loved one can't be replaced.

You can find love again.

Take time to think ....*It is the source of power*

Take time to play ....*It is the secret of perpetual youth*

Take time to read .... *It is the fountain of wisdom*

Take time to pray ....*It is the greatest power on earth*

Take time to love and be loved......*It is a God-given privilege*

Take time to be friendly ....*It is the road to happiness*

Take time to laugh........................*It is the music of the soul*

Take time to give............................*It is too short a day to be selfish*

Take time to work ....*It is the price of success*

Take time to save ....*It is the foundation of your future*

Answers to Questions Everyone ASKS ...

Here they are...answers from the experts

A's for arthritis;

B's the bad back,

C's the chest pains, Perhaps car-di-ac?

D is for dental decay and decline,

E is for eyesight, can't read that top line!

F is for fissures and fluid retention,

G is for gas, which I'd rather not mention.

H is high blood pressure --I'd rather it be low;

I is for incisions with scars you can show.

J is for joints, out of socket, won't mend,

K is for knees that crack when they bend.

L is for libido, what happened to sex?

M is for memory, I forget what comes next.

N is neuralgia, in nerves way down low;

O is for osteo, the bones that don't grow!

P is for prescriptions, I have quite a few; just give me a pill and I'll be good as new!

Q is for queasy, is it fatal or flu?

R is for reflux, one meal turns to two.

S is for sleepless nights, counting my fears,

T is for Tinnitus; there're bells in my ears!

U is for urinary; big troubles with flow;

V is for vertigo, that's "dizzy," you know.

W is for worry, NOW what's going 'round?

X is for X ray, and what might be found.

Y is another year I've left behind,

Z is for zest that I still have-in my mind

I've survived all the symptoms, my body's deployed. And I'm keeping 26 doctors fully employed!

This chapter answers the questions many others have asked.

1. **How soon after or long after a death must an individual be buried?**

   The time before burial varies by state so check with your local funeral director. It takes time to secure all permits and authorizations, to notify family and friends, to prepare the cemetery site and comply with religious considerations. Some states have limitations on the maximum length of time allowed to pass prior to final disposition. Consult your local funeral provider for applicable regulations.

2. **Does a body have to be embalmed before it is buried?**

   No. Embalming is not required for burial. Embalming may depend on such factors as whether the family has selected a public viewing with an open casket or to enhance the deceased's appearance for a private family viewing. Embalming will probably be required if the body is going to be transported by air or rail, or because, for many reasons, time must pass before burial.

3. **What are the principal types of cemeteries, and how do they differ?**

   There are two broad categories of cemeteries: traditional cemeteries and memorial parks or gardens. A traditional cemetery usually has upright stone monuments. Many traditional cemeteries also have private mausoleums for above ground interment. Because traditional cemeteries have functioned in a community for hundreds of years, they typically contain a lot of history, such as architecture, statuary history and other art. Cemeteries often feature lush landscaping and impressive greenery.

   Memorial parks and gardens are a newer type of cemetery. Featured are burial plots without tombstones. Markers in the parks and gardens often are bronze memorials that are placed level with the ground to blend with the beauty of the landscape. They often feature expansive lawns with a variety of trees, flowering beds and gardens, as well as fountains, sculpture or memorial architecture. Some cemeteries have both traditional upright monument sections and garden sections. Both types of cemeteries may offer above ground interment in community mausoleums.

Both traditional cemeteries and memorial parks may be operated on a for-profit or not-for-profit basis. They may be owned by an individual or by a corporation. Some are owned mutually, and many are the property of towns, counties and religious or fraternal groups. Both may have chapels, crematories, community mausoleums, mortuaries or funeral homes and columbariums.

4. What are my choices in ground burial?

Most common are single graves and lots for two or more graves. Not all types of graves are available at all cemeteries. If you want an unusual burial plot, start by asking the cemetery administration.

5. How do I choose the right type of grave?

There are lots of things to consider, like:

- What type of memorial do you want? Some markers are set flat on the ground and some are upright monuments.
- How many persons will be buried in the place you choose?
- How much do you want to spend? Graves vary by size, location and price.

6. What are the other options?

Many cemeteries offer interment in lawn crypts, entombment in mausoleums, a niche in a columbarium, or interment in an urn space. Some cemeteries provide choices for those who have chosen cremation. For example, some facilities now provide for scattering of remains in a garden set aside exclusively for cremated ashes. If that option is chosen, a plaque memorializing the deceased can be placed in the area.

7. Why would I want my cremated remains to be placed in a columbarium or interred or scattered at the cemetery? Why shouldn't I just have them scattered in the sea or in some other place of my choosing?

As long as you are in compliance with local regulations, your cremated remains can be scattered in any place that is meaningful to you. However, your choice may present difficulties for your survivors who may find it hard to pour your mortal remains onto the ground or into the ocean. To avoid conflict, discuss your wishes ahead of time with those who will actually have to do the scattering.

Another difficulty with scattering can occur if the remains are disposed of in an anonymous, unmarked, or public place. Access to the area may subsequently be restricted, or undeveloped land may be developed, or any of a host of other conditions may arise that could make it difficult for your survivors to visit the site to remember you.

If your cremated remains are scattered in your back yard, what happens if your survivors relocate sometime in the future? Once scattered, cremated remains cannot easily be collected back up. Having your remains placed, interred, or scattered on a cemetery's grounds enables future generations to have a place to go to remember. Survivors then will have a place to visit that will always be maintained and preserved.

8. Why is having a place to visit so important?

Psychologists say that remembrance practices, from the funeral or memorial service to permanent memorialization, serve an important emotional function for survivors by helping to bring closure and allowing the healing process to begin. Providing a permanent resting place for the deceased is a dignified treatment for a loved one's mortal remains, and fulfills the natural human desire for memorialization.

9. What is opening and closing and why is it so expensive?

Opening and closing fees can include 50 or more separate services provided by the cemetery. Examples of the services provided include the fee for opening and closing the grave; administration and permanent recordkeeping *(determining ownership, obtaining permission, the completion of other documentation in the interment register, and maintaining all legal files)*; opening and closing the grave *(locating the grave and laying out the boundaries, excavating and filling the interment space)*; installation and removal of the lowering device;

placement and removal of artificial grass dressing and coco matting at the grave site, leveling, tamping, re-grading and sodding the grave site and leveling and re-sodding the grave if the earth settles.

10. Can we dig our own grave to avoid the charge for opening and closing?

No. The actual opening of the grave and closing of the grave is just one component of the opening and closing fee. Because of safety issues which arise around the use of machinery on cemetery property and the protection of property of adjacent interment rights' holders, the actual opening and closing of the grave is done by cemetery grounds personnel.

11. What are burial vaults and grave liners?

These are the outside containers into which the casket is placed. Burial vaults are designed to protect the casket and may be made of a variety of materials including concrete, stainless steel, galvanized steel, copper, bronze, plastic or fiberglass. A grave liner is a lightweight version of a vault which simply keeps the grave surface from sinking in.

12. Must I purchase a burial vault?

In most areas of the country, state or local law does not require that you buy a container to surround the casket in the grave. However, many cemeteries require that you have such a container so that the ground will not sink. Either a grave liner or a burial vault will satisfy these requirements.

13. What happens when a cemetery runs out of land?

When a cemetery runs out of land, it will continue to operate and serve the community. Most states have laws that require funds to be set aside from each sale for the long-term care and maintenance of the cemetery.

14. What is "double depth?"

Many cemeteries either allow for the burial of two caskets in a grave or have specific sections where this type of grave is available. Double depth means that one casket is placed in the grave deeply enough so that when a second interment is required, the second casket can be placed on top of the first casket.

15. How much do graves cost, and why aren't they priced the same all over?

Grave prices can really vary. Grave prices are normally dependent on their location. Graves in urban centers are more expensive than in rural centers because of the replacement value of land. Within the cemetery, grave prices can vary by the section in which the grave is located.

16. What is entombment?

Entombment is the interment of human remains in a tomb or mausoleum. It involves placing a casket or cremation urn in a crypt or niche *(individual compartment within a mausoleum or columbarium)* which is then sealed.

17. What is a mausoleum?

Historically, the word mausoleum comes from the large temple-like structure which was erected by Queen Artemisia in the ancient city of Harlicarnassua as the final resting place for her late husband, King Mausolus. Mausolus, from which the word mausoleum is derived, ruled over Caria in Asia Minor and died in 353 B.C. His mausoleum is now regarded as the fifth of the Seven Wonders of the World.

A community mausoleum is simply a large building designed to provide above ground entombment for a number of people. Sharing the costs of the mausoleum with other individuals makes it more affordable than a private mausoleum.

18. What are the advantages of a mausoleum burial?

Mausoleum crypts are both clean and dry. They offer a viable alternative for those who have an aversion to being interred in the ground. Furthermore, with the growing shortage of available land for cemetery use, mausolea allow for a maximum number of entombments in a minimum amount of space.

19. Aren't mausoleums only for rich people?

In most cases, the cost of mausoleum entombment is comparable to the costs of interment in a lot with an upright monument.

20. Are there different types of crypts?

Yes. Single crypts are designed for one entombment only. There are three different kinds of double crypts: tandem crypts permit two entombments lengthwise in a crypt; companion crypts permit two entombments side-by-side; Westminster crypts permit two entombments, the first below floor level, and the second above it. Most mausolea are built five, six and seven crypts high. The price of the crypt will depend on its location and the type of crypt. For example, upper level crypts are usually less expensive than those located at eye level.

21. What is a columbarium?

A columbarium, often located within a mausoleum or chapel, is constructed of numerous small compartments (niches) designed to hold urns containing cremated remains.

22. What happens to a mausoleum if there is an earthquake?

Modern mausoleums are steel-reinforced concrete structures, covered with granite or marble. They typically are built to meet all local building specifications, including those regarding earthquakes.

23. How does a mausoleum protect the body?

Because the casket is placed in a clean, dry, above ground crypt, the remains are protected from water and the elements of the earth.

24. Can you actually see the bodies in a mausoleum?

No. When you visit a mausoleum, you see the front of the crypt, which typically is made of granite or marble. The name of the person who has died, along with their years of birth and death, appear on the crypt front. The casket rests behind a solid, sealed panel which is placed behind the granite or marble crypt front.

25. How many people will a crypt hold?

Crypts come in several sizes. Although "singles" and "doubles" are the most common, some crypts can accommodate up to four caskets.

26. What is a tandem?

A tandem is a mausoleum space designed to accommodate two caskets lengthwise.

27. How can a mausoleum help eliminate expenses?

When you select a mausoleum, you eliminate the need for expensive vaults and monuments or memorials, which almost always are purchased with ordinary earth burial.

28. What are lawn crypts?

Lawn crypts are essentially underground tombs, constructed of reinforced concrete, steel and waterproof materials.

29. What is the difference between lawn crypts and double depth burial spaces?

Lawn crypts are pre-set. Double depth burial lots are set at the time of death.

30. May I make the necessary arrangements in advance?

Yes, usually all arrangements may be made in advance.

31. What happens if I buy cemetery property and later move to another area?

Many cemeteries now belong to credit exchange programs which allow for a dollar-for-dollar transfer of services and merchandise between participating cemeteries.

32. When I buy a grave do I receive a deed just like when I purchase other types of real estate?

When you purchase a grave you are in fact purchasing the right to designate who may be interred in the space, rather than purchasing the grave itself, which remains the property and responsibility of the cemetery. You also have a right to place a memorial where permitted.

33. What is endowment care?

A portion of the purchase price of the grave is contributed to an endowment care fund for the regular care and maintenance of the cemetery. Regular care and maintenance activities can include: cutting grass, re-grading of graves, planting and caring for trees, maintenance of water supply systems, roads, drainage, etc. The minimum amount to be contributed to the endowment care fund is normally governed by law.

34. What guarantee do I have that endowment care will take care of the cemetery?

While not guaranteed, endowment care funds are very conservatively managed. Income from the fund can only be spent on care and maintenance of the cemetery – the capital is not touched. In most states, consumer protection laws govern endowment care funds.

35. Can I resell my grave?

It really depends on the rules and regulations of the cemetery and the laws of the state or province. While some cemeteries will repurchase graves, others have laws restricting the resale to a third party.

36. Is cemetery property tax deductible?

No, the purchase of a grave is not tax-deductible, although the charitable donation of unwanted grave spaces may be deductible as an "in kind" charitable contribution.

37. Will a cemetery ever be used for something else? Can the bodies be moved and buildings built?

Communities afford respect to cemeteries and to the memorialization which cemeteries provide and have strict rules governing the use of cemetery lands. Graves are normally considered to be sold in perpetuity, which restricts possible redevelopment.

38. In a hundred years will this cemetery still be here?

Cemetery lands are thought of as being in perpetuity. There are cemeteries throughout the world that have been in existence well over hundreds of years.

39. What is a disinterment? What is the process, and why does it happen?

Disinterment is the removal of the casket containing human remains from a grave. Disinterment may be ordered by certain public officials without the consent of the grave owner or the next of kin. Individuals or families may also request disinterment, if for example, they would like to have the human remains relocated to another grave.

40. What does the government give a veteran as a grave marker?

The United States government provides headstones and markers for the graves of veterans and eligible dependents anywhere in the world which are not already marked. Flat bronze, flat granite, flat marble and upright marble types are available to mark the grave of a veteran or dependent in the style consistent with existing monuments at the place of burial. Bronze niche markers are also available to mark columbaria in national cemeteries used for interment of cremated remains.

41. If I am a veteran and plan to be buried in a national cemetery, is my spouse eligible to be buried next to me?

Yes, a space for your spouse or any other minor children can be authorized at the time of your death.

Note: Many of the answers were provided by funeral or memorial associations

Final EXAM...

Highlights from all the chapters

A minister was completing a temperance sermon. With great emphasis he said, "If I had all the beer in the world, I'd take it and pour it into the river."

With even greater emphasis, he said, "And if I had all the wine in the world, I'd take it and pour it into the river."

And then, finally, shaking his fist in the air, he said, "And if I had all the whiskey in the world, I'd take it and pour it into the river." Sermon complete, he sat down.

The hymn-leader stood and announced with a smile, nearly laughing, "For our closing hymn, let us sing Hymn No.365, 'Shall We Gather at the River.'"

Well, this is the finish. Although this chapter is titled "Final Examination," the real final exam is yet to come. *(You have to die to pass!)* This chapter includes questions that, by now, you should have answers to. *(Maybe you don't have all the answers yet, but you are working on them. Right?)* Every one of the questions in this chapter is discussed *(not necessarily answered)* in the preceding chapters. Treat the questions like an exam or a To Do List.

At this time in your life, what are the most important things to do as you recognize and prepare for the fact that your death is inevitable . . . eventually?

I've asked many groups that question. Pretty generally, these are the priorities they've set *(the listing is a compilation, so listing order is not significant):*

Write my will

Decide whether to be buried or cremated

Prepare advance directives or 5 Wishes directive

Prepare an Instant Action document

Write a loving letter to my survivors

Plan my funeral/memorial service

These are the "hot" to-do items. There are a lot more specific things listed below.

There's a lot of work involved in getting ready to die, isn't there? I've discovered as I talk with seniors, there always seems to be something I've neglected to mention. Let me hear from you if there's a topic that should have been included in this book. Email me at: *jlesliesr@sbcglobal.net*

You're not dead yet. So get on with doing the things you've got to do!

QUESTIONS AND YOUR ANSWERS

Selected an attorney to help with your will?

Prepared your Instant Action documents?

Stored copies of your Instant Action form in places like your Going Away book, the glove box of your car, on your person, in your house, with a friend, with a son or daughter, your agents, or your attorney?

Prepared a loving letter to accompany your will?

Prepared your will, using an attorney recommended by others?

Decided what you want done with your body after you die?

Started getting rid of items of no value or of little value?

Started a list of garage/estate/yard sale items to be sold after your death and how the money will be divided among those you specify? (*These are items **not included** in your will.*)

Started a list of valuable and not so valuable possessions to be given away after your death, including their stories, if appropriate,and decided how you're going to give them away? (*These are items **not included** in your will.*)

Started a list of the **really** valuable possessions to be given away and their stories, if appropriate, and decided how you're going to give them away. (*These are items **included** in your will.*)

Started writing the stories about your life, significant events you want remembered, and other topics of lasting importance?

Started discussing your "going away" activities with your family?

Decided, of the Advance Directives listed below, which you want to use and started preparing them?

- Medical Power of Attorney
- Directive to Physicians and Family or Surrogates
- Out-of-Hospital Do-Not-Resuscitate Order
- Declaration for Mental Health Treatment

Chosen to use the "5 Wishes" directive?

Planned your funeral/memorial service, answering questions like these:

Minister?	Location of service?
Open/closed casket?	Music?
Scriptures?	Poems?
Eulogies?	Special activities?
Etc.	

Created a list of your "Most Important" documents and started putting them in your Going Away book?

Decided on special things you want to do before you die and begun doing them?

Developed Important Personal Information About Yourself to pass on?

Identified people to be notified of your death?
        Immediately by phone
        By email
        By letter

Developed Important Other Medical Information?

Written your Loving Letter?

Written Your Obituary or, at least, outlined it or identified the events you want put into your obituary?

Written your Personal Going Away Party instructions?

Decided the kind of care you want as your health deteriorates?

Written a Letter of Permission regarding your care *(different from Advance Directives)*?

Developed your family genealogy?

Created a time line of your major life events?

Recorded your medical history?

Decided on the significant events in your life and written their stories?

Recorded the medicines you take?

Written your doctors' names and contact information?

Decided how you want to be treated in your last days?

Decided how things are to be divided among your heirs?

Annually updated your will?

Created and named your Going Away book?

Decided on the contents of your Going Away book ?

Started putting things in all the sections of your book?

Told others about your Going Away book and where you keep it?

Discussed your will with your family?

Accepted a reasonable guess of your life expectancy?

Started writing your story *(your biography)*?

Written the story of your family?

Begun developing the costs of various burial/cremation alternatives?

Made "end of life" choices for either burial, cremation, or giving your body to science?

Planned the events you want after your funeral/memorial service?

Planned your funeral/memorial service?

Decided where you want your obituary to be published?

Understood the Signs of Dying?

Forgiven everybody, including yourself?

Developed an understanding of the importance of a dying person saying goodbye?

Thought about how you'll say goodbye?

Determined how you will decide you should no longer live independently?

Chosen a lifestyle for your old age?

Revisited and updated your legacy statements?

Decided where your funeral/memorial service will be held?

Thought how you will process your grief at the death of a loved one?

Thought about how you would respond to your family's notice you are "slipping a little?"

Told your family about your end-of-life preferences?

Created an emergency fund to handle immediate expenses after your death?

Arranged for a cosignor on your emergency funds account?

Named your executor?

Authorized others to sign checks and have access to your strong box?

Chosen an open or closed casket?

Created medical documents to carry in your wallet or purse and in the glove compartment of your car?

Thought about the evidences of your Christian legacy?

Thought about the evidences of your legacy of Godly character?

Thought about the evidences of your legacy of possession?

Created a special occasion for someone you love?

Learned to do the things your companion has done for years without your help?

Understood the complexity of the dying process?

Accepted the Christian belief that a realistic view of death is an affirmation of your faith?

Thought about the words you would use when talking with a friend or loved one who is dying?

Accepted your "Funeral Rights" and made relevant decisions?

Addressed your fears regarding your death?

Decided that Hospice is an option in your final days, and have you told others how you feel about using this service?

DID YOU PASS THE EXAM?

Since you've come this far, it's obvious you're not dead. However, you can't hide from the inevitable fact you are on a journey that will end, and that you will, someday, die. And, if you're like most of the others who have participated in this journey, you still have a lot of stuff to do.

This book will help.

It starts with you accepting responsibility for the final period of your life. Take charge. Start doing the things you really want to do. Decide what you want to occur in the period right before your death, plan the final celebration of your life, make it clear how you want your estate distributed, and, finally, leave a legacy of love.

Do these things and you will be at peace.

To repeat a little: although there has always been a lot of variety and excitement in your life, and you wish it would go on forever, there comes a time when it won't. So, leave no doubt with your loved ones about your state of mind. Let your family know how you want to be treated in the last days of your life. Don't just talk about it; put it all in writing and file it in your Going Away book. And, of course, leave your book in a place where it can easily be found.

Talk to your loved ones enough that they will have an understanding of your desires. Don't leave them wondering. But don't talk **too** much.

If you're lucky, before you die you'll be able to say goodbye to those you care about. Just in case life's end sneaks up on you, leave clear instructions about everything: your end-of-life care, burial or cremation choice, funeral or memorial preferences, the disposition of your possessions, and be sure to leave a letter with your will that leaves no doubt about the love you had for your family and others.

It all finally comes down to this: don't take life too seriously; no one gets out alive. Be a good person. Follow the guidelines in this book.

Your survivors will thank you, and you'll be a legend.

5680148R0

Made in the USA
Charleston, SC
20 July 2010